UNCOVERING THE UNCONSCIOUS BIAS

A PRACTICAL GUIDE FOR MANAGERS TO CREATE A PSYCHOLOGICALLY SAFE AND INCLUSIVE WORKPLACE

KARISHMA MANCHANDA

Made with ❤ on the Notion Press Platform
www.notionpress.com

The book is dedicated to my darling daughter, Raabhya who made me open my eyes to the unconscious bias, operating as an undercurrent in a woman's life, much of which is carried to the workplace, whether consciously or unconsciously by the beings of our society.

Contents

Foreword

"Until we uncover and confront our own unconscious biases, we remain trapped in a cycle of perpetuating the very inequalities we seek to eliminate. Only by shining a light on our hidden beliefs and assumptions can we create a truly inclusive and psychologically safe workplace."

Preface

Personal childhood experiences and dysfunctional family dynamics can have a significant impact on an individual's mindset and behaviour, particularly in the workplace. These experiences can shape an individual's beliefs and attitudes towards themselves and others, as well as their ability to form and maintain healthy relationships.

One way in which childhood experiences can affect an individual's mindset is through the development of negative self-perception and self-esteem. Individuals who have experienced emotional or physical abuse, neglect, or other forms of trauma during childhood may struggle with feelings of worthlessness and insecurity, which can carry over into adulthood. This can lead to difficulties in forming and maintaining healthy relationships, both personally and professionally.

Another way in which childhood experiences can affect an individual's mindset is through the development of coping mechanisms that may be detrimental in the workplace. For example, individuals who have experienced trauma or abuse may develop a tendency to avoid confrontation or to suppress their emotions, which can make it difficult for them to effectively communicate and collaborate with their colleagues.

Dysfunctional family dynamics can also have a significant impact on an individual's mindset and behaviour. For example, individuals who have grown up in households where there is a lack of emotional support or where communication is poor may struggle with trust issues and difficulty forming healthy relationships. This can make it difficult for them to form effective working relationships with their colleagues, especially if they are not aware of the root cause of their difficulties.

Personal childhood experiences can play a significant role in shaping an individual's attitudes and beliefs towards gender, which can lead to gender bias in the workplace.

For example, individuals who have grown up in households where traditional gender roles were strictly enforced may have internalized the belief that men and women should occupy different roles and have different responsibilities. This can lead to unconscious biases in the workplace, where individuals may make assumptions about the capabilities and qualifications of their colleagues based on their gender.

Similarly, individuals who have experienced abuse or neglect at the hands of a parent or caregiver of a specific gender may develop negative associations with that gender, leading to biases and prejudices in their interactions with colleagues of that gender.

Individuals who have experienced trauma or dysfunction in their families may also develop coping mechanisms that can negatively impact their interactions with colleagues of a specific gender. For instance, an individual may avoid or suppress their emotions when interacting with colleagues of the same gender as their abuser, which can make it difficult for them to effectively communicate and collaborate.

Additionally, the lack of representation and diversity in the workplace can also contribute to gender bias. For example, in fields where one gender is underrepresented, unconscious biases may be reinforced, leading to discrimination against members of that gender in the hiring process and the workplace.

These issues can also manifest in the form of gender-based biases, with individuals who have experienced childhood trauma or dysfunction in their families being more likely to hold sexist or misogynistic attitudes. This can create a rift between genders in the workplace, leading to a lack of trust and cooperation among colleagues, which can negatively impact productivity and morale.

The effects of personal childhood experiences and dysfunctional family dynamics on an individual's mindset and behaviour can also be exacerbated by societal factors such as discrimination and marginalization. For example, individuals who belong to marginalized communities may have experienced additional traumas or stresses that can further impact their mental and emotional well-being.

Furthermore, these experiences can also lead to a lack of representation and diversity in the workplace. Individuals from marginalized communities who have experienced childhood traumas or dysfunctions in their families may be less likely to pursue careers in certain fields, leading to a lack of diversity in certain industries.

In addition, employers and managers can also take steps to promote an inclusive and diverse workplace, much of which is covered in subsequent chapters of this book, by providing training on unconscious bias and actively recruiting and promoting individuals from marginalized communities.

Overall, personal childhood experiences and dysfunctional family dynamics can have a significant impact on an individual's mindset and behaviour, particularly in the workplace. It is important for employers and managers to be aware of these potential issues and to take steps to support and empower their employees, to create a more inclusive and productive work environment.

Gender bias in the workplace can lead to exclusion in a variety of ways.

First, when individuals hold unconscious biases or stereotypes about the capabilities and qualifications of individuals based on their gender, they may make assumptions and decisions that lead to exclusion. For example, if a manager believes that women are less capable of holding leadership positions, they may not consider them for promotions or leadership roles. This can lead to a lack of representation and opportunities for individuals of that gender.

Second, gender bias can also lead to microaggressions and hostile work environments. Microaggressions are subtle, often unintentional actions or statements that can be hurtful or offensive to members of a specific group. For example, a colleague who makes sexist jokes or comments, or who consistently interrupts or talks over a female colleague, may create a hostile work environment for women. This can lead to feelings of isolation and exclusion for individuals who are targeted by these microaggressions.

Third, gender bias can also lead to discrimination in the hiring process. For example, if employers or managers hold unconscious biases about the capabilities and qualifications of individuals based on their gender, they may be less likely to hire or promote individuals of that gender. This can lead to a lack of representation and opportunities for individuals of that specific gender.

Overall, gender bias in the workplace can lead to exclusion by creating barriers to representation, and opportunities, and creating a hostile environment for individuals of a specific gender. It is important for employers and managers to be aware of these potential issues and to take steps to promote an inclusive and diverse workplace, by providing training on unconscious bias, actively recruiting, and promoting individuals from marginalized communities, and creating a culture where microaggressions and discrimination will not be tolerated.

There are several benefits of gender inclusion to a business.

First, a diverse workforce can lead to better decision-making and problem-solving. When individuals with different backgrounds, experiences, and perspectives are included, a wide range of ideas and perspectives are brought to the table, which can lead to more innovative solutions and better decision-making.

Second, gender inclusion can improve employee engagement and retention. When employees feel that they are valued and respected, they are more likely to be engaged and motivated in their work. This can lead to increased productivity and employee retention.

Third, gender inclusion can improve the company's reputation and customer base. Companies that are seen as inclusive and diverse are often viewed more favourably by customers, which can lead to increased brand loyalty and customer satisfaction.

Fourth, gender inclusion can also help a company to tap into new markets and customer bases. Having a diverse workforce can help a company to better understand and connect with customers from different backgrounds and cultures, which can be especially beneficial for companies that operate in a global market.

Fifth, gender inclusion can help to reduce the gender pay gap. When women and other underrepresented groups have equal access to opportunities, it can lead to greater pay equity and reduce the gender pay gap.

Overall, gender inclusion can bring many benefits to a business, such as better decision-making, improved employee engagement and retention, improved reputation, and customer base, tapping into new markets and customer bases, and reducing the gender pay gap. It is important for employers and managers to be aware of these potential benefits and to take steps to promote an inclusive and diverse workplace for all genders.

Creating an inclusive and psychologically safe workplace can bring many benefits to managers.

First, an inclusive and psychologically safe workplace can lead to better decision-making and problem-solving. When employees feel that they are valued and respected, they are more likely to speak up and share their ideas, which can lead to more innovative solutions and better decision-making.

Second, an inclusive and psychologically safe workplace can improve employee engagement and retention. When employees feel that they are part of a supportive and inclusive team, they are more likely to be engaged and motivated in their work, which can lead to increased productivity and employee retention.

Third, an inclusive and psychologically safe workplace can improve the company's reputation and customer base. Companies that are seen as inclusive and supportive are often viewed more favourably by customers, which can lead to increased brand loyalty and customer satisfaction.

Fourth, an inclusive and psychologically safe workplace can help to reduce the gender pay gap. When women and other underrepresented groups have equal access to opportunities and feel included and respected in the workplace, it can lead to greater pay equity and reduce the gender pay gap.

Fifth, creating an inclusive and psychologically safe workplace can help managers to foster a culture of trust and collaboration among employees, which can improve communication and teamwork and help to overcome conflicts and challenges more efficiently.

Overall, creating an inclusive and psychologically safe workplace can bring many benefits for managers, such as better decision-making, improved employee engagement and retention, improved reputation and customer base, reducing the gender pay gap, and fostering a culture of trust and collaboration. It is important for managers to be aware of these potential benefits and to take steps to promote an inclusive and supportive environment for all employees.

So, we see that there are several benefits of creating a safe and inclusive workplace where all genders can thrive.

This book is crafted with the intent to make managers realize how our personal childhood experiences and dysfunctional family dynamics plague our mindset and create a rift between various genders at the workplace.

The book also provides valuable resources for managers and employers to unearth unconscious bias and tools to mitigate the impact of unconscious bias in the workplace.

CHAPTER ONE

The Basics

Diversity at the workplace refers to the variety of differences among the employees of an organization. These differences can be based on various characteristics such as race, ethnicity, gender, age, religion, ability, sexual orientation, and education, among others. A workplace that values diversity recognizes, respects, and celebrates the unique backgrounds, experiences, and perspectives of all its employees. Such an environment can lead to increased creativity, innovation, and collaboration, as well as a more positive and inclusive culture.

Having a diverse workforce can bring a range of perspectives and approaches to problem-solving, which can be beneficial for the organization. It can also lead to a better understanding and connection with customers and clients from diverse backgrounds.

A diverse workplace can also be more representative of the community and society in which the organization operates, which can help improve the public image and reputation of the company.

However, achieving diversity in the workplace is not always easy, and it requires intentional effort and commitment from leadership and all employees. It is important to create an inclusive culture that values and respects differences and actively works to eliminate any biases or discrimination.

There are various ways organizations can promote diversity in the workplace, such as through inclusive recruitment and hiring practices, providing diversity training and education, and implementing policies and programs that support diversity and inclusion.

It is also important for organizations to be aware of and address any issues or challenges that may arise concerning diversity, such as discrimination or unequal treatment of certain groups.

Gender Diversity at Workplace

Gender diversity refers to the range of gender identities and expressions that exist within a given community or society. It includes people who identify as male, female, or nonbinary, as well as those who may identify as genderqueer, genderfluid, or agender. Gender diversity acknowledges that gender is a spectrum and that people can and should be able to express their gender in a way that feels authentic to themselves. It also involves creating an inclusive and accepting environment for people of all gender identities and expressions.

Gender diversity is an important aspect of diversity and inclusion in many settings, including schools, workplaces, and social groups. It involves creating an environment where people of all gender identities and expressions feel welcome, valued, and supported.

Gender diversity can be challenging to achieve in societies where there are rigid expectations about how people should look, act, and behave based on their gender. These expectations, known as gender roles, can make it difficult for people to express their gender in a way that feels authentic to themselves.

Promoting gender diversity involves challenging and dismantling systems of oppression and discrimination that limit people's ability to fully express their gender. This may include advocating for policies and practices that support transgender and nonbinary people, such as inclusive bathroom and locker room policies or the option to use preferred gender pronouns.

Gender diversity is important because it allows people to be their authentic selves and live their lives freely and fully. It also helps to create more inclusive and accepting communities and societies where everyone can thrive.

Inclusion at Workplace

Inclusion refers to the practice of actively involving and welcoming people who may be marginalized or underrepresented in each context. It involves creating an environment where everyone feels valued, respected, and supported, and where their unique needs and experiences are recognized and considered. Inclusion is an important aspect of diversity and helps to create a sense of belonging and community.

Inclusion can take many forms, depending on the context. For example, in the workplace, it may involve creating policies and practices that are inclusive of people with disabilities, people of different cultural and ethnic backgrounds, and people of different gender identities and expressions. In schools, it may involve creating inclusive classrooms and curricula that recognize and respect the diversity of students' experiences and backgrounds. In social groups and organizations, it may involve making sure that everyone feels welcome and included in activities and events.

Overall, inclusion involves recognizing and celebrating the unique qualities and differences that each person brings to a community or organization and actively working to create a welcoming and inclusive environment for everyone.

Gender Inclusion at Workplace

Gender inclusion at the workplace refers to creating an environment where people of all gender identities and expressions feel valued, respected, and supported. It involves making sure that policies and practices are inclusive of transgender and nonbinary people, and that there is a culture of acceptance and inclusion for people of all genders.

There are several ways to promote gender inclusion in the workplace, including:

- Offering equal opportunities and treatment to people of all genders. This includes things like equal pay for equal work, equal access to training and development opportunities, and equal representation in leadership and decision-making roles.
- Providing inclusive facilities and resources, such as gender-neutral bathrooms and locker rooms, and making sure that all employees have access to the facilities they need to express their gender comfortably and safely.
- Using inclusive language and pronouns and making sure that all employees feel comfortable using their pronouns.
- Encouraging open communication and dialogue about gender diversity and inclusion and creating a safe space for people to ask questions and express themselves.
- Providing resources and support for employees who are transitioning, such as access to healthcare and counselling services.

- Overall, promoting gender inclusion in the workplace involves creating a culture of acceptance and respect for all gender identities and expressions and actively working to dismantle systems of oppression and discrimination that limit people's ability to fully express their gender.

But, much of the ability to create an inclusive workplace is slaughtered by the undercurrents the unconscious bias. These unconscious biases are mental shortcuts that people use to make sense of the world around them. These biases can influence our perceptions, behaviours, and decisions in ways that are often outside of our awareness. Uncovering unconscious bias helps people to become more aware of these biases and how they can impact their interactions with others. The goal of this training is to help people make more conscious, thoughtful, and equitable decisions.

Unconscious biases can have a significant impact on the workplace, and they can lead to problems such as discrimination, inequality, and a lack of diversity and inclusion. Uncovering the unconscious bias for managers can help to address these issues by increasing awareness of the existence and impact of unconscious biases and by providing tools and strategies for reducing their influence.

Managers play a critical role in shaping the culture and policies of an organization and uncovering unconscious bias can help them to create a more inclusive and equitable work environment. It can also help managers to make more fair and unbiased decisions, which can lead to better outcomes for employees and the organization as a whole.

Overall, uncovering unconscious bias can be an important tool for promoting diversity, inclusion, and fairness in the workplace.

Here are the top five reasons for training managers on managing their unconscious bias in the workplace:

- **To promote diversity and inclusion:**

Unconscious biases can lead to a lack of diversity and inclusivity in the workplace, which can have negative impacts on both employees and the organization. Training can help managers to recognize and overcome their biases and create a more inclusive work environment.

- **To make more fair and unbiased decisions:**

Unconscious biases can influence the decisions that managers make, leading to unfair treatment of some employees. Training can help managers to become more aware of their biases and make more objective and unbiased decisions.

- **To improve employee performance and satisfaction:**

A workplace that is free from the negative impacts of unconscious bias can be a more positive and productive environment for employees. Training can help managers to create a more supportive and fair work environment, which can lead to improved performance and satisfaction among employees.

- **To foster a positive company culture:**

Unconscious biases can contribute to a toxic or negative company culture. Training can help managers to create a more positive and supportive culture that promotes the well-being and success of all employees.

- **To reduce the risk of discrimination lawsuits:**

Unconscious biases can lead to discrimination, which can result in legal issues for the organization. Training can help managers to avoid discriminatory practices and reduce the risk of discrimination lawsuits.

CHAPTER TWO

The Bias

What is a Bias?

This is the most common question and yet least thought about when it comes to addressing the question, "Am I operating from a biased state of perception?". Let us discover what it truly means and how often we encounter it in a day to day life, yet remain unaware of our biased approach to self, to others, and to life in general.

A bias is a tendency or inclination, especially one that interferes with impartial judgment. Biases can be positive or negative, and they can influence how a person thinks, acts, or makes decisions.

Biases can have a significant impact on how we perceive and interact with the world around us, and they can lead to unfair treatment or discrimination against certain groups of people. It is important to be aware of our own biases and to try to overcome them to be fairer and more unbiased in our thoughts, actions, and decisions.

Bias is defined as a disproportionate weight in favour of or against an idea or thing, usually in a way that is closed-minded, prejudicial, or unfair.

Biases can be innate or learned. People may develop biases for or against an individual, a group, or a belief.

Effect of Bias on Gender Inclusion in the Workplace

Bias can affect gender inclusion in the workplace in several ways. For example:

If a person has a bias against people of a certain gender, they may be less likely to hire, promote, or support people who are affected by that bias. This can lead to a lack of diversity and inclusion in the workplace.

Bias can also affect how people are treated and perceived in the workplace. For example, a person who is biased against people of a certain gender may be more likely to view their work as inferior or to overlook their contributions and achievements.

Bias can also lead to a lack of understanding or awareness of the unique needs and experiences of people of different genders. For example, a person who is biased against transgender or nonbinary people may not understand or be sensitive to their needs, such as the need for inclusive bathroom facilities.

Overall, it is important to be aware of and challenge biases to create a more inclusive and supportive workplace environment for people of all genders. This may involve creating policies and practices to address and prevent discrimination and bias and providing training and resources to help employees understand and overcome their biases.

Types of Bias:

Intentional Vs Unintentional Bias:

Bias can be either intentional or unintentional.

Intentional bias refers to cases where a person deliberately acts in a discriminatory or biased manner. This might involve consciously choosing to exclude or discriminate against a particular group of people or making decisions based on stereotypes or prejudices rather than on objective criteria.

Unintentional bias, also known as **unconscious bias**, refers to cases where a person holds biases or stereotypes without being aware of them. These biases can influence a person's thoughts, actions, and decisions in subtle ways, and may even conflict with a person's conscious values and beliefs. Unconscious bias can be difficult to recognize and overcome, but it is important to be aware of it and try to challenge it.

It is important to recognize and challenge both intentional and unintentional bias to create a more inclusive and equitable environment. This may involve creating policies and practices to address and prevent discrimination and bias, as well as providing training and resources to help people understand and overcome their biases.

Both intentional and unintentional bias can have negative impacts on gender inclusion in the workplace. **Some potential impacts include:**

- **Exclusion or discrimination**: Bias can lead to the exclusion or discrimination of people based on their gender, which can create a hostile or unwelcoming environment for some employees.
- **Inequality**: Bias can also contribute to inequality in the workplace, such as unequal pay or opportunities for advancement
- **Limited representation:** Bias can lead to a lack of representation of people of certain genders in leadership positions in certain fields.
- **Negative stereotypes:** Bias can also perpetuate negative stereotypes about people of certain genders, which can impact how they are perceived and treated in the workplace.

- **Limited understanding**: Bias can lead to a lack of understanding or awareness of the unique needs and experiences of people of different genders, which can make it difficult to create an inclusive and supportive environment for all employees.

Here are some examples of intentional and unintentional bias in the workplace:

Example of Intentional bias:

A manager deliberately excludes people of a certain gender from a job opportunity or promotion because they do not believe that they are capable or qualified.

Another example could be a company that has a policy of only hiring people of a certain gender or race.

Often witnessed in a typical workplace which is not sensitive to inclusion is a colleague who makes derogatory or offensive comments about people of a certain gender or sexual orientation.

Examples of Unintentional bias:

A manager assumes that a job candidate is more qualified because they attended a prestigious university, even though they may not have relevant experience or skills. This is an example of the "halo effect," which is a type of unconscious bias that occurs when a person's overall positive impression of someone influences their judgment of that person's characteristics.

Another example can be a colleague who consistently interrupts or talks over people of a certain gender during meetings, without realizing that they are doing so. This is an example of microaggressions, which are subtle forms of discrimination that can be unconscious and unintentional.

A manager assumes that an employee is not interested in a leadership role because they are introverted, even though introversion is not necessarily correlated with leadership ability. This is an example of the "fundamental attribution error," which is a type of unconscious bias that occurs when a person attributes someone's behaviour or characteristics to their personality rather than to external factors.

Challenging and overcoming bias is an important step in creating a more inclusive and equitable workplace for people of all genders. This may involve creating policies and practices to address and prevent discrimination and bias, as well as providing training and resources to help employees understand and overcome their biases.

Explicit vs. Implicit Bias:

Explicit bias refers to conscious attitudes or beliefs that a person holds about a particular group of people. These biases are openly and overtly expressed, and the person is aware of their biases.

Implicit bias, on the other hand, refers to unconscious attitudes or beliefs that a person holds about a particular group of people. These biases are not openly expressed and may even conflict with a person's conscious values and beliefs. Implicit biases can influence a person's thoughts, actions, and decisions in subtle ways, and a person may not even be aware that they hold these biases.

It is important to be aware of both explicit and implicit biases, as they can both have negative impacts on our thoughts, actions, and decisions. It is also important to try to challenge and overcome both types of bias to be fairer and more unbiased in our thoughts, actions, and decisions.

Here are some examples of implicit and explicit bias against women in the workplace:

Examples of Implicit bias:

A manager who consistently interrupts or talks over women during meetings, without realizing that they are doing so. This is an example of microaggressions, which are subtle forms of discrimination that can be unconscious and unintentional.

A colleague assumes that a woman is not interested in a leadership role because she is caring and nurturing, even though these qualities are not necessarily correlated with leadership ability. This is an example of stereotype threat, which is a type of unconscious bias that occurs when a person feels at risk of confirming a negative stereotype about their group.

A company that has a policy of only hiring people who are recent college graduates, which disproportionately affects women who may have taken time off to care for children or other family members. This is an example of structural bias, which refers to the systemic barriers and discrimination that can disadvantage certain groups.

Having understood implicit biases, let us also consider a few examples of explicit bias:

Manager deliberately excludes women from job opportunities or promotions because they do not believe that they are capable or qualified.

Another case of explicit bias expression can be of a colleague who makes derogatory or offensive comments about women.

A company that has a policy of only hiring men for certain positions, such as a sales job.

Conscious Vs Unconscious Bias:

A **conscious bias** refers to attitudes or beliefs that a person holds consciously and is aware of. These biases are openly and overtly expressed, and the person is aware of their biases.

An **unconscious bias**, also known as an implicit bias, refers to attitudes or beliefs that a person holds unconsciously. These biases are not openly expressed and may even conflict with a person's conscious values and beliefs. Unconscious biases can influence a person's thoughts, actions, and decisions in subtle ways, and a person may not even be aware that they hold these biases.

It is important to be aware of both conscious and unconscious biases, as they can both have negative impacts on our thoughts, actions, and decisions. It is also important to try to challenge and overcome both types of bias to be fairer and more unbiased in our thoughts, actions, and decisions.

Here are some examples of conscious and unconscious bias against women in the workplace, starting with the conscious bias:

Manager deliberately excludes women from promoting them to leadership roles because they do not believe that women can handle the responsibilities and stress that comes with holding such a position.

Another case can be of a colleague who makes derogatory or offensive comments about women.

Now, let us consider a few examples of unconscious bias:

A manager who consistently interrupts (manterrupting) or talks over women during meetings, without realizing that they are doing so. This is an example of microaggressions, which are subtle forms of discrimination that can be unconscious and unintentional.

A colleague assumes that a woman is not interested in a leadership role because she is caring and nurturing, even though these qualities are not necessarily correlated with leadership ability. This is an example of stereotype threat, which is a type of unconscious bias that occurs when a person feels at risk of confirming a negative stereotype about their group.

A company that has a policy of only hiring people who are recent college graduates, which disproportionately affects women who may have taken time off to care for children or other family members. This is an example of structural bias, which refers to the systemic barriers and discrimination that can disadvantage certain groups.

Now that we have understood the basics of bias in the workplace and how it rolls out in an organization even without malicious intent, let us give deeper to understand why bias takes place and how can we become more aware of our actions and behaviours that violate inclusion in the workplace.

Diving Deeper into Bias at the Workplace:

Bias refers to a systematic deviation from impartiality or objectivity, often resulting from preconceived notions or stereotypes. Bias can manifest in various forms, such as cognitive, social, and cultural bias. Understanding these various forms of bias can help individuals and organizations to become aware of their own biases, and to take steps to mitigate their impact.

Many different types of bias can influence our thoughts, actions, and decisions. Some common forms of bias include most of which fall under cognitive bias.

Cognitive biases are mental shortcuts or tendencies to think in certain ways that can lead to distorted or irrational thinking. It refers to the mental shortcuts that people use to make judgments and decisions, which can lead to distorted or inaccurate perceptions. These biases include things like confirmation bias, where people tend to look for information that confirms their existing beliefs and overlook information that contradicts them.

Social bias refers to how people are treated differently based on their group membership, such as race, gender, age, or sexuality. Social biases can lead to discrimination and exclusion in the workplace, as well as impact the ability of a business to make fair and unbiased decisions.

Cultural bias refers to the cultural beliefs and practices that can shape our perceptions, attitudes, and behaviour. For example, cultural bias can lead to stereotypes and assumptions about people from different cultures, which can lead to discrimination and misunderstanding.

By understanding these various forms of bias, individuals and organizations can become more aware of their own biases and take steps to mitigate their impact. This can lead to more inclusive and equitable workplaces, as well as more accurate and fair decision-making.

When we become aware of which bias we tend to operate with, it becomes easier for us to recognise and then course correct. With this intent, let us now dive deeper into various forms of biases that prevail in the workplace.

The Framing Effect:

The framing effect is a type of cognitive bias that occurs when how information is presented influences a person's judgment or decision-making. The framing effect can have significant impacts on how people perceive and interpret events and information, and it can lead to biased or irrational decisions.

For example, consider a company that is considering two job candidates, one of whom is a man and the other a woman. If the man is described as "assertive" and the woman as "bossy," the framing effect may lead people to perceive the man as more qualified or suitable for the job, even though the two candidates may have similar qualifications and experiences. Similarly, if a woman is described as "ambitious" while a man is described as "driven," the framing effect may lead people to perceive the man as more competent or suitable for the job.

The framing effect can have significant impacts on bias against women in the workplace. By influencing how people perceive and interpret information about women, the framing effect can contribute to stereotypes and biases that can create barriers to advancement and equality for women. It is important to be aware of the framing effect and to try to overcome it to be fairer and more unbiased in our thoughts, actions, and decisions.

The Sunk Cost Bias:

The sunk cost bias is a type of cognitive bias that occurs when a person continues investing time or resources in something because of the effort that has already been invested, even if it is not rational or productive to do so. The sunk cost bias can lead people to persist in activities or projects that are not likely to be successful, simply because they have already invested a lot of time, money, or other resources into them.

For example, a person might continue working on a project that is not likely to be successful because they have already invested a lot of time and effort into it, even though it would be more rational to cut their losses and move on to something else. Or a person might continue attending a course or workshop that is not helpful or relevant to their goals because they have already paid for it, even though it would be more efficient to stop attending and use the time and resources for something else.

The sunk cost bias can be a significant barrier to change and progress, as it can lead people to persist in activities or projects that are not productive or beneficial. It is important to be aware of the sunk cost bias and to try to overcome it to make more rational and productive decisions.

The Anchoring Bias:

Anchoring bias is a form of cognitive bias. This is the tendency to rely too heavily on the first piece of information that one encounters, even if it is not relevant or accurate.

For example, a colleague who has heard a negative rumour about a woman's performance may anchor on that rumour and use it to evaluate the woman's work, even if they have no first-hand experience or evidence to support the rumour.

Group Think or Conformity Bias:

Conformity bias, also known as groupthink, is a type of bias that occurs when a group prioritizes agreement and conformity over critical thinking and decision-making. Conformity bias can lead to the suppression of dissenting opinions and the exclusion of minority voices, and it can have negative impacts on diversity and inclusion.

For example, a group of colleagues who consistently exclude women from decision-making or leadership roles, even though they are qualified and capable because they do not want to "rock the boat" or challenge the status quo, exhibit conformity bias. Similarly, a team that values conformity and collaboration over individuality and creativity may discourage women from speaking up or taking risks, leading to a lack of diversity and inclusion.

It is important to recognize and challenge conformity bias to create a more inclusive and supportive workplace environment. This may involve creating policies and practices that encourage diversity of thought and the inclusion of minority voices, as well as providing training and resources to help people understand and overcome conformity bias.

These are biases that affect how people perceive and interact with members of a particular group. Examples include in-group bias (a preference for people who are like oneself) and out-group bias (prejudice against people who are different from oneself).

Groupthink is a type of bias that occurs when a group prioritizes agreement and conformity over critical thinking and decision-making. Groupthink can have negative impacts on diversity and inclusion, as it can lead to the suppression of dissenting opinions and the exclusion of minority voices.

Here are some examples of groupthink bias against women in the workplace:

A group of colleagues consistently exclude women from decision-making or leadership roles, even though they are qualified and capable because they do not want to "rock the boat" or challenge the status quo.

A group of managers who overlook or dismiss the ideas and suggestions of women because they do not fit with the group's preconceived notions or assumptions.

A team that values conformity and collaboration over individuality and creativity, which may discourage women from speaking up or taking risks.

It is important to recognize and challenge groupthink to create a more inclusive and supportive workplace environment for women. This may involve creating policies and practices that encourage diversity of thought and the inclusion of minority voices, as well as providing training and resources to help people understand and overcome groupthink bias.

Stereotypes:

These are oversimplified or inaccurate beliefs about a particular group of people. Stereotypes can influence how a person thinks and acts towards members of that group.

Here are some examples of stereotypes about women that can occur in the workplace:

- Women are not as competent as men.
- Women are more emotional or irrational than men.
- Women are not interested in leadership roles.
- Women are only interested in "feminine" careers, such as Human Resource Management
- Women are more interested in work-life balance and are not as committed to their careers as men.
- Women are more sensitive or easily offended than men.

These stereotypes can influence how women are perceived and treated in the workplace, and they can create barriers to advancement and equality. It is important to challenge and overcome these stereotypes to create a more inclusive and equitable environment for women in the workplace.

Affinity Bias:

An affinity bias, also known as a similarity bias or a homophily bias, is a type of bias that occurs when a person is more drawn to or more favourably disposed towards people who are like themselves. This can include similarities in characteristics such as age, race, ethnicity, gender, sexual orientation, religion, or educational background.

Affinity bias can influence a person's thoughts, actions, and decisions in several ways. For example, a person with an affinity bias may be more likely to hire, promote, or support people who are like themselves, even if they are not the most qualified candidates. Affinity bias can also lead to a lack of diversity and inclusion in teams and organizations, as people with similar characteristics may be more likely to be drawn to and welcomed in certain environments.

It is important to be aware of and challenge affinity bias to create a more inclusive and equitable environment. This may involve creating policies and practices to address and prevent bias, as well as providing training and resources to help people understand and overcome their biases.

Here are some examples of affinity bias against women in the workplace:

A manager is more likely to hire, promote, or support women who are like themselves (e.g., the same age, race, or educational background) even if they are not the most qualified candidates.

A team that is more welcoming and supportive of women who are like most of the team (e.g., the same age, race, or educational background), while being less welcoming or supportive of women who are different.

A company that has a culture that is more welcoming and supportive of women who are like most of the company (e.g., the same age, race, or educational background), while being less welcoming or supportive of women who are different.

It is important to be aware of and challenge affinity bias to create a more inclusive and equitable environment for women in the workplace. This may involve creating policies and practices to address and prevent bias, as well as providing training and resources to help people understand and overcome their biases.

Confirmation Bias:

Confirmation bias is a type of cognitive bias that refers to the tendency to seek out and interpret information that confirms one's existing beliefs or biases. Confirmation bias can lead people to selectively pay attention to and remember information that supports their beliefs while ignoring or discounting information that does not.

For example, a person who has a belief that women are not as competent as men may seek out examples of women who are not successful in their careers and use them to confirm their bias while ignoring or dismissing examples of successful women.

Similarly, a person who has a belief that women are more emotional or irrational than men may pay more attention to instances where women are emotional or irrational and use them to confirm their bias while ignoring instances where men are emotional or irrational.

Confirmation bias can have significant impacts on diversity and inclusion, as it can lead people to ignore or dismiss evidence that challenges their beliefs or biases. It is important to be aware of the confirmation bias and to try to overcome it to be fairer and more unbiased in our thoughts, actions, and decisions.

Here are some examples of confirmation bias against women in the workplace:

A manager who has a belief that women are not as competent as men may seek out examples of women who are not successful in their careers and use them to confirm their bias while ignoring or dismissing examples of successful women.

A colleague who has a belief that women are more emotional or irrational than men may pay more attention to instances where women are emotional or irrational and use them to confirm their bias while ignoring instances where men are emotional or irrational.

A company that has a policy of only promoting people who have a certain level of experience may overlook or dismiss the qualifications of women who have taken time off to care for children or other family members, even if they have relevant skills and experience. This is an example of the "motherhood penalty," which refers to the negative impacts that motherhood can have on a woman's career.

It is important to be aware of the confirmation bias and to try to overcome it to be fairer and more unbiased in our thoughts, actions, and decisions. This may involve actively seeking out information that challenges our beliefs and biases, as well as being open to the idea that external factors and circumstances can have a significant impact on people's behaviour.

Attribution Bias:

An attribution bias is a type of cognitive bias that refers to the tendency to attribute the behaviour or characteristics of an individual or group to their inherent personal characteristics, rather than to external factors or circumstances.

Attribution biases can lead to stereotypes and prejudices, as they can influence how we perceive and interpret the actions and behaviours of others.

There are several different types of attribution biases, including:

- **Fundamental attribution error:** This is the tendency to overestimate the impact of personal characteristics and underestimate the impact of situational factors in explaining other people's behaviour. For example, a person might attribute a woman's success to her intelligence and hard work, rather than to factors such as supportive colleagues or access to resources.

- **Self-serving bias:** This is the tendency to attribute one's successes to personal characteristics and abilities while attributing one's failures to external factors.
- **Actor-observer bias:** This is the tendency to attribute one's behaviour to situational factors while attributing the behaviour of others to personal characteristics.

It is important to be aware of attribution biases and to try to overcome them to be fairer and more unbiased in our thoughts, actions, and decisions. This may involve considering multiple explanations for the actions and behaviours of others and being open to the idea that external factors and circumstances can have a significant impact on people's behaviour.

Gender Bias:

Gender bias refers to prejudice or discrimination based on a person's gender. Gender bias can manifest in several ways, including:

- **Stereotypes:** Oversimplified or inaccurate beliefs about a particular group of people based on their gender.
- **Discrimination:** Different treatment of people based on their gender can lead to unequal opportunities or outcomes.
- **Harassment:** Unwanted or inappropriate behaviour is directed at a person based on their gender.
- **Sexual Harassment:** While the Government of India has a separate Act on Sexual Harassment of Women at Workplace (Prevention, Prohibition and Redressal) Act, 2013, it is worth noting that much of this is an outburst of gender bias which prevails at the workplace.

Gender bias can occur in a variety of settings, including the workplace, education, and healthcare. It can have significant impacts on people's lives and opportunities, and it can create barriers to equality and inclusion. It is important to recognize and challenge gender bias to create a more equitable and inclusive society.

Gender Bias in India:

There are many forms of gender bias in India that can impact women's lives and opportunities. Some examples include:

- Stereotypes and cultural expectations restrict women's roles and opportunities in society, such as the expectation that women should prioritize marriage and child-rearing over education or work.
- Unequal access to education, healthcare, and other resources, can limit women's opportunities and choices.
- Harassment and violence against women, including sexual harassment, domestic violence, and honour killings.
- Discrimination in the workplace, including the "glass ceiling" that can prevent women from advancing to leadership roles, and the "motherhood penalty," which refers to the negative impacts that motherhood can have on a woman's career, including discrimination in hiring and promotions and the expectation that women will take on a disproportionate share of caregiving responsibilities.

It is important to recognize and challenge these forms of gender bias to create a more equitable and inclusive society for women in India. This may involve creating policies and practices to address and prevent gender bias, as well as providing education and resources to help people understand and overcome their biases.

The Halo Effect:

The halo effect is a type of cognitive bias that occurs when a person's overall impression of a person or thing influences their evaluations of that person or thing's specific characteristics or attributes. The halo effect can lead to biased or irrational judgments, as it can cause people to overlook or downplay negative information and exaggerate positive information.

For example, if a person has a positive overall impression of a colleague, they may be more likely to overlook or downplay any negative traits or behaviours that the colleague exhibits, and to exaggerate their positive traits or behaviours.

Similarly, if a person has a negative overall impression of a product, they may be more likely to overlook or downplay any positive features or benefits of the product, and to exaggerate its negative features or drawbacks.

The halo effect can have significant impacts on decision-making and judgment, and it is important to be aware of it to avoid letting it influence our thoughts and actions. This may involve actively seeking out and considering multiple sources of information and being open to the possibility that our overall impressions may be biased or incomplete.

The Horn Effect:

The horn effect is a type of cognitive bias that is the opposite of the halo effect. While the halo effect occurs when a person's overall impression of a person or thing influences their evaluations of that person or thing's specific characteristics or attributes in a positive way, the horn effect occurs when a person's overall impression of a person or thing negatively influences their evaluations.

For example, if a person has a negative overall impression of a colleague, they may be more likely to overlook or downplay any positive traits or behaviours that the colleague exhibits, and to exaggerate their negative traits or behaviours. Similarly, if a person has a positive overall impression of a product, they may be more likely to overlook or downplay any negative features or drawbacks of the product, and to exaggerate its positive features or benefits.

Like the halo effect, the horn effect can have significant impacts on decision-making and judgment, and it is important to be aware of it to avoid letting it influence our thoughts and actions. This may involve actively seeking out and considering multiple sources of information and being open to the possibility that our overall impressions may be biased or incomplete.

As humans, we tend to associate one experience negatively, we safely assume that all our experiences with the other gender or people with similar gender will yield the same halo or horny results – which may not be true.

Each person is unique and so are their or personal situation, circumstances and values. It is unjust and unsafe to generalize successes and failures across all people of similar gender or diversity segments.

The Contrast Effect:

The contrast effect is a type of cognitive bias that occurs when the perception of a person or thing is influenced by the context in which it is presented. The contrast effect can lead people to perceive things as better or worse than they are, based on the relative context in which they are presented.

For example, if a person is shown a series of job candidates and one candidate stands out as particularly qualified or impressive, the contrast effect may lead the person to perceive the other candidates as less qualified or impressive in comparison. Similarly, if a person is shown a series of products and one product stands out as particularly high-quality or innovative, the contrast effect may lead the person to perceive the other products as lower-quality or less innovative in comparison.

The contrast effect can have significant impacts on judgment and decision-making, and it is important to be aware of it to avoid letting it influence our thoughts and actions. This may involve actively seeking out and considering multiple sources of information and being aware of the context in which information is presented.

How Does 'Bias' Affect the workplace?

Bias can have several negative impacts on the workplace, including:

Impact of Bias on Organizational Branding:

Bias can hurt an organization's branding, which is the reputation and image that the organization projects to its customers, clients, and stakeholders.

When people feel that they are being unfairly treated or that they are not being given equal opportunities because of their race, gender, age, sexual orientation, or other characteristics, it can lead to negative perceptions of the organization and damage its reputation.

This can lead to a lack of trust and loyalty among customers, clients, and stakeholders, and can impact the organization's bottom line.

On the other hand, when people feel that they are being treated fairly and that they have equal opportunities, they are more likely to have positive perceptions of the organization and to speak positively about it to others.

This can enhance the organization's reputation and lead to increased trust and loyalty among customers, clients, and stakeholders, which can have a positive impact on the organization's bottom line.

Organizations need to recognize and address bias to create a more inclusive and equitable workplace that has a positive brand and that can attract and retain customers, clients, and stakeholders. This may involve creating policies and practices to address and prevent bias, as well as providing education and resources to help people understand and overcome their biases.

Impact of Bias on Revenue and Growth of Organization:

Bias can hurt an organization's revenue and growth. When people feel that they are being unfairly treated or that they are not being given equal opportunities because of their race, gender, age, sexual orientation, or other characteristics, it can lead to a lack of engagement and a decreased sense of belonging and connection to the organization.

This can lead to decreased motivation, productivity, and innovation, which can impact the organization's bottom line.

On the other hand, when people feel that they are being treated fairly and that they have equal opportunities, they are more likely to feel a sense of belonging and connection to the organization. This can lead to increased motivation, productivity, and innovation, which can have a positive impact on the organization's bottom line.

Organizations need to recognize and address bias to create a more inclusive and equitable workplace that fosters growth and success. This may involve creating policies and practices to address and prevent bias, as well as providing education and resources to help people understand and overcome their biases.

Impact of Bias on Attracting Talent:

Bias can hurt an organization's ability to attract talent and successfully recruit new employees. When people feel that they are being unfairly treated or that they are not being given equal opportunities because of their race, gender, age, sexual orientation, or other characteristics, it can lead to negative perceptions of the organization and damage its reputation.

This can make it harder for the organization to attract top talent and can lead to a lack of diversity and inclusion within the organization.

On the other hand, when people feel that they are being treated fairly and that they have equal opportunities, they are more likely to have positive perceptions of the organization and to speak positively about it to others.

This can enhance the organization's reputation and make it a more attractive place to work, leading to increased diversity and inclusion.

Organizations need to recognize and address bias to create a more inclusive and equitable workplace that can attract top talent and successfully recruit new employees. This may involve creating policies and practices to address and prevent bias, as well as providing education and resources to help people understand and overcome their biases.

Impact of Bias on Employee Engagement & Morale:

Bias can hurt employee growth and career advancement. When people feel that they are being unfairly treated or that they are not being given equal opportunities because of their race, gender, age, sexual orientation, or other characteristics, it can create barriers to advancement and limit their career opportunities.

On the other hand, when people feel that they are being treated fairly and that they have equal opportunities, they are more likely to feel a sense of belonging and connection to the organization and to be motivated to grow and advance in their careers.

Organizations need to recognize and address bias to create a more inclusive and equitable workplace that supports employee growth and career advancement. This may involve creating policies and practices to address and prevent bias, as well as providing education and resources to help people understand and overcome their biases.

Impact of Bias on Equality at the Workplace:

Bias can lead to unequal treatment of people based on characteristics such as gender, race, ethnicity, sexual orientation, religion, or age, which can create barriers to advancement and create a lack of diversity and inclusion.

Impact of Bias on Poor Decision-Making:

Bias can distort people's perceptions and lead to flawed or irrational decision-making, which can have negative consequences for the organization and its employees.

Bias can have a significant impact on decision-making. Bias is a natural human tendency, and it is difficult to eliminate it. However, it is important to be aware of the potential for bias and to take steps to minimize its influence on decision-making.

Bias can distort people's perceptions and lead to flawed or irrational decision-making. It can cause people to overlook or downplay important information or to give too much weight to certain types of information. This can lead to poor decisions that have negative consequences for the organization and its stakeholders.

Organizations need to create processes and practices that help to minimize the impact of bias on decision-making. This may involve seeking out and considering multiple sources of information, seeking input and feedback from diverse perspectives, and being open to the possibility that our own biases may be influencing our decision-making. It may also involve providing education and resources to help people understand and overcome their biases.

Impact of Bias on Productivity:

Bias and discrimination can create a toxic or unwelcoming work environment, which can lead to decreased morale, engagement, and productivity.

Bias and discrimination can hurt productivity in the workplace. When people feel that they are being unfairly treated or that they are not being given equal opportunities because of their race, gender, age, sexual orientation, or other characteristics, it can lead to decreased morale, engagement, and motivation. This can result in decreased productivity and a lack of commitment to the organization.

On the other hand, when people feel that they are being treated fairly and that they have equal opportunities, they are more likely to feel a sense of belonging and connection to the organization and to be motivated to work to their full potential. This can lead to increased productivity and a sense of commitment to the organization.

Organizations need to recognize and address bias to create a more inclusive and equitable workplace that fosters productivity. This may involve creating policies and practices to address and prevent bias, as well as providing education and resources to help people understand and overcome their biases.

Impact of Bias on Legal Consequences:

Bias and discrimination can lead to legal consequences for organizations, such as lawsuits or fines.

Bias and discrimination can have legal consequences in India. The Indian Constitution prohibits discrimination on the grounds of religion, race, caste, sex, or place of birth (Article 15), and various laws have been enacted to give effect to this prohibition and to protect the rights of disadvantaged groups.

For example, the Equal Remuneration Act, of 1976 prohibits discrimination in the payment of wages based on gender, and the Sexual Harassment of Women at Workplace (Prevention, Prohibition, and Redressal) Act, 2013 prohibits sexual harassment of women at the workplace and provides for the establishment of Internal Complaints Committees to address complaints of sexual harassment.

In India, the Rights of Persons with Disabilities Act, of 2016 prohibits discrimination against people with disabilities, including unconscious discrimination. The act defines disability broadly, covering physical, mental, intellectual, and sensory impairments, and recognizes the rights of people with disabilities to equality, dignity, autonomy, and full participation in society.

The act also provides for measures to promote and protect the rights of people with disabilities, including accessibility, reasonable accommodations, and affirmative action. It requires public buildings, transport systems, and information and communication technologies to be made accessible to people with disabilities, and mandates the creation of grievance redressal mechanisms to address complaints of discrimination and violation of rights.

Overall, the act is an important step towards promoting the inclusion and empowerment of people with disabilities in India, and towards creating a more equitable and just society.

Violations of these laws can result in legal consequences for organizations, such as fines or legal action. Organizations need to recognize and address bias and discrimination to avoid legal consequences and to create a more inclusive and equitable workplace.

This may involve creating policies and practices to address and prevent bias and discrimination, as well as providing education and resources to help people understand and overcome their biases.

We have seen how gender inclusion plays a significant role in promoting innovation in the workplace which is key to business growth and success. We have also seen through these brainstorming exercises how much implicit and unconscious bias still prevails in our work relationships.

There are many other ways in which bias takes place in an organization.

Apart from gender bias, discrimination and bias also prevails for persons with disabilities and transger persons.

Here are **some ways in which biases against people with disabilities (PwD)** that can be observed in the workplace, amongst many others:

- **Prejudice and stereotypes**: Many people hold negative attitudes toward PwD and often view them as incompetent, helpless, and dependent.
- **Physical barriers**: The physical environment of the workplace, such as stairs, narrow doorways, and inaccessible restrooms, may create barriers that prevent PwD from participating fully in the workplace.

- **Limited job opportunities**: PwD may face barriers in accessing job opportunities, such as limited recruitment efforts, lack of accommodations during the interview process, and discriminatory hiring practices.
- **Negative perceptions about productivity**: Employers may hold negative stereotypes about the productivity of PwD, such as assuming that they will require more time off or accommodations, or that their work will be of lower quality.
- **Unequal pay:** PwD may experience wage discrimination due to their disability, which can result in lower pay for the same work as non-disabled workers.
- **Lack of training and professional development:** Employers may overlook the need for training and professional development opportunities for PwD, which can limit their career growth and advancement.
- **Limited social inclusion:** PwD may experience social isolation in the workplace due to attitudes and biases that prevent them from being fully included in the workplace culture and social activities.

It is important to recognize and address these biases to create a more inclusive and equitable workplace for all employees, including those with disabilities. Here are some examples of each type of bias against PwD in the workplace:

Prejudice and Stereotypes:

- Assuming that a person with a physical disability is unable to perform certain tasks, without considering their individual abilities and skills.
- Stereotyping PwD as less intelligent, less competent, or less productive than non-disabled workers.

- Assuming that PwD are not interested in pursuing ambitious career goals or leadership roles.
- Assuming that PwD need more time off or accommodations than non-disabled workers, without considering their individual needs.
- Viewing PwD primarily as beneficiaries of charity or social welfare programs, rather than as capable and independent workers.

Physical Barriers:

- A workplace with steps or stairs that are inaccessible to employees who use wheelchairs or other mobility aids.
- A workplace with narrow doorways or hallways that are difficult for employees with mobility impairments to navigate.
- Restrooms that are not designed or equipped to accommodate employees with mobility impairments.
- Workspaces that are not adjustable or adaptable to meet the needs of employees with different physical abilities.
- Lack of accessible parking spaces or transportation options to the workplace.

Limited Job Opportunities:

- Failure to advertise job openings in accessible formats, such as Braille or large print.
- Lack of accessibility features during the application process, such as closed captioning on video interviews or alternative text for images.
- Discriminatory hiring practices, such as rejecting a candidate solely on the basis of their disability, without considering their qualifications or job performance.

- Failing to provide reasonable accommodations during the interview process, such as an interpreter or accessible transportation.
- Unconscious biases that affect recruitment and hiring, such as assuming that a PwD is not the "right fit" for the company culture.

Negative Perceptions about Productivity:

- Assuming that a PwD will be absent from work more frequently or for longer periods than non-disabled workers.
- Assuming that a PwD will require more supervision or support than non-disabled workers, without considering their individual abilities and skills.
- Assuming that a PwD will be slower or less efficient in completing tasks than non-disabled workers, without considering their individual accommodations and supports.
- Failing to recognize the contributions and achievements of PwD in the workplace, and assuming that their successes are due solely to their disability status.
- Overemphasizing the challenges and limitations of PwD, rather than recognizing their strengths and potential as workers.

Unequal Pay:

- Paying PwD less than non-disabled workers for the same job, without a justifiable reason.
- Denying PwD the opportunity for bonuses or other forms of compensation available to non-disabled workers, without a justifiable reason.

- Offering PwD jobs with lower wages or fewer benefits, without a justifiable reason.
- Making assumptions about the financial needs of PwD based solely on their disability status, and adjusting their pay accordingly.
- Failing to provide equal pay for equal work, regardless of disability status.

Lack of Training and Professional Development:

- Failing to provide training and development opportunities that are accessible to PwD, such as online courses with closed captioning or accessible training materials.
- Failing to provide training on how to work with and accommodate PwD in the workplace, which can limit their career growth and advancement.
- Failing to recognize the unique skills and perspectives that PwD bring to the workplace, and failing to provide training or development opportunities that leverage those strengths.
- Failing to provide reasonable accommodations that would enable PwD to participate in training and development opportunities, such as interpreters or assistive technology.
- Making assumptions about the career aspirations of PwD based solely on their disability status, without providing them with necessary support.

And just like the PwDs experiece bias, members from other communities such as that of the transgender persons.

Here are some **examples of biases against transgender persons** that can appear in the workplace, along with examples of each type of bias as experienced by transgender persons in an organization in India:

Prejudice and Stereotypes:

- Assuming that transgender persons are mentally unstable or deviant, and therefore unsuitable for the workplace.
- Stereotyping transgender persons as sexual predators or perverts, based on misconceptions about their gender identity.
- Assuming that all transgender persons are involved in sex work or other illegal activities, based on harmful stereotypes.
- Stereotyping transgender persons as not fitting into the gender binary, and therefore not suitable for binary gendered jobs.
- Assuming that transgender persons are not professional, disciplined or responsible workers, based solely on their gender identity.

Discriminatory Policies and Practices:

- Workplace policies that discriminate against transgender persons, such as dress codes that only permit male/female attire or policies that prohibit the use of preferred names or pronouns.
- Discriminatory hiring practices, such as not considering transgender persons for employment or excluding them from the recruitment process altogether.
- Denying transgender persons access to workplace facilities, such as restrooms or changing rooms, based on their gender identity.

- Failing to provide reasonable accommodations for transgender persons, such as appropriate uniforms, flexible work hours or job duties that better suit their gender identity.
- Failure to provide adequate healthcare benefits or coverage for transgender persons, including access to gender-affirming surgeries and hormone therapy.

Harassment and Bullying:

- Verbal or physical abuse directed at transgender persons, including the use of derogatory slurs or discriminatory language.
- Social exclusion or ostracism of transgender persons, leading to feelings of isolation and stigmatization.
- Workplace bullying directed at transgender persons, including public humiliation, belittling or intimidating behavior.
- Refusal by coworkers or managers to use the correct pronouns or names when referring to transgender persons, causing distress and feelings of invalidation.
- Sexual harassment and assault, which transgender persons may be at a higher risk of experiencing due to their gender identity.

Limited Job Opportunities:

- Lack of employment opportunities for transgender persons, due to discriminatory hiring practices and societal prejudice.
- Limited job options available for transgender persons, especially in binary gendered jobs where they may not be accepted or may face hostility.

- Lack of career advancement opportunities for transgender persons, due to prejudice and bias against their gender identity.
- Transgender persons may face limited job prospects, especially in traditional or conservative fields, such as finance, law, or medicine.
- Lack of access to education, training and development opportunities, leading to limited career choices and opportunities.

Unequal Treatment and Pay:

- Transgender persons may be paid less than their cisgender counterparts for the same job, based on discriminatory attitudes and beliefs.
- Unequal treatment of transgender persons in terms of job duties, job assignments, promotions, and other aspects of employment.
- Transgender persons may be denied benefits and leave entitlements, such as maternity or paternity leave, based on their gender identity.
- Lack of access to medical benefits or coverage, leading to financial difficulties and health complications.
- Transgender persons may be denied equal access to retirement and pension benefits, based on their gender identity.

It is important to recognize and address these biases to create a more inclusive and equitable workplace for all employees, including transgender persons. There are several other types of bias that can be observed in Indian organizations. Here are some examples:

- **Caste Bias**: Caste is a significant social issue in India, and unfortunately, it is also prevalent in the workplace. Many employers tend to have biases based on caste, which can result in discrimination against employees from certain castes. This can lead to unfair treatment, limited career opportunities, and unequal pay.
- **Age Bias**: Ageism is a form of bias that can be seen in Indian organizations. Older workers may be overlooked for promotions or job opportunities, and younger employees may be undervalued due to their lack of experience. Stereotypes about older or younger workers can also lead to unfair treatment.
- **Regional Bias**: India is a diverse country with many different regions, each with its own culture and language. Unfortunately, this diversity can sometimes lead to regional bias in the workplace. Employees from certain regions may be viewed as less capable or less qualified than others, based on stereotypes or biases.
- **Religious Bias**: Religious bias is another form of bias that can be seen in Indian organizations. Employees from certain religions may face discrimination or be treated unfairly based on their religious beliefs or practices. This can impact their job opportunities, work assignments, and relationships with colleagues.
- **Language Bias**: India has many different languages, and this can sometimes lead to language bias in the workplace. Employees who do not speak the dominant language of the workplace may be viewed as less capable or less intelligent, which can lead to unfair treatment and limited job opportunities.

It is important for employers to recognize these biases and take steps to address them in the workplace. Creating a more inclusive and equitable workplace can benefit everyone and lead to a more productive and positive work environment.

In the subsequent chapters, we will understand why does 'bias' occur in the first place?

CHAPTER THREE

The Neuro- Psychology Hidden Behind Our Biases

Neuropsychology helps us to understand how the brain and nervous system affect the ways we think, act, and behave. It studies the relationships between the brain, the rest of the nervous system, and various aspects of behaviour and cognition, including perception, attention, memory, language, and emotion.

By understanding how the brain and nervous system influence behaviour, neuropsychologists can help to identify and treat problems that may arise because of brain injuries or disorders. For example, a neuropsychologist may work with an individual who has suffered a stroke to assess the impact of the stroke on cognitive and behavioural functioning and to develop strategies to help the individual compensate for any deficits.

In addition, the study of neuropsychology can help us to better understand how our thoughts, emotions, and behaviours are influenced by the brain and nervous system. This can help us to develop more effective ways of coping with stress, managing our emotions, and making decisions, among other things.

What is Neuropsychology?

Neuropsychology is a branch of psychology that focuses on the relationships between the brain and behaviour. It is a scientific field that uses a variety of methods, including brain imaging techniques and cognitive and behavioural assessments, to study the brain and how it functions.

Neuropsychology affects the ways we think, act, and behave. Neuropsychology suggests that our beliefs and biases may be influenced by the structure and function of our brains.

For example, research has shown that the amygdala, a part of the brain involved in processing emotions and making decisions, also plays a role in the formation of biases and stereotypes.

Studies have found that when people are exposed to stimuli that elicit a negative emotional response (e.g., images of people from a different racial group), the amygdala becomes more active. This suggests that the amygdala may be involved in the formation of negative biases and stereotypes.

Other research has suggested that how information is processed in the brain may also influence the formation of beliefs and biases. For example, studies have found that people are more likely to form biased beliefs when they are exposed to information that is presented in a biased or selective manner, rather than when they are exposed to a more balanced or neutral presentation of the information.

There is a strong relationship between the way our brain processes external stimuli coming from our environment, especially during the early childhood and developmental stages, which serves as the basis of all our beliefs and biases

It defines the way we operate as adults based on the formation and maintenance of these mental constructs.

Role of Early Child Development in Integrated-Biases in Adulthood:

Early child development plays a significant role in shaping our beliefs and behaviours. The experiences and environments that children are exposed to during their early years can have a lasting impact on their cognitive, emotional, and social development.

For example, research has shown that children who grow up in supportive and nurturing environments are more likely to develop positive beliefs about themselves and the world around them.

They may be more confident, resilient, and able to cope with stress and challenges. On the other hand, children who grow up in environments that are neglectful or abusive may be more likely to develop negative beliefs about themselves and the world and may be more prone to anxiety, depression, and other mental health issues.

In addition, early childhood development can also shape our beliefs about others and the world around us. Children who are exposed to diverse environments and people from an early age may be more open-minded and accepting of differences, while children who are not exposed to such diversity may be more prone to developing biases and stereotypes.

Overall, children need to have supportive and nurturing environments during their early years to promote healthy development and the formation of positive beliefs.

Early childhood development can affect our gender bias in several ways. For example:

- Children may learn gender stereotypes from the people around them. If they are exposed to gender-stereotyped toys, activities, and expectations, they may internalize those stereotypes and believe that certain activities, behaviours, and interests are "appropriate" for boys or girls.
- Children may also learn about gender roles and expectations from their parents and other adults in their lives. If children see their parents or other adults reinforcing traditional gender roles and expectations, they may adopt those views and beliefs as their own.
- Children may also develop gender biases based on their own experiences and interactions with people of different genders. If they have negative experiences with people of a certain gender, they may develop biases against that gender.
- Children may also learn about gender biases through media and other cultural influences. If they are exposed to media that reinforces gender stereotypes or portrays people of certain genders negatively or stereotypically, they may internalize those biases.

Overall, children need to be exposed to diverse environments and perspectives during their early years to promote open-mindedness and reduce the risk of developing gender biases.

Schemas and Bias:

A schema is a cognitive framework or mental structure that helps us to organize and make sense of information. It is a way of organizing and categorizing knowledge in our minds and helps us to understand and remember new information about what we already know.

For example, if you have a schema for dogs, you might have information about what dogs look like, what they do, and how they behave. When you encounter a new dog, you can use this schema to help you understand and remember information about the dog, such as its breed, size, and temperament.

Schemas can be especially useful for helping us to process and understand new information. However, they can also lead to biases and stereotypes if they are based on incomplete or inaccurate information. For example, if your schema for dogs is based on negative experiences with a few aggressive breeds, you may have a biased view of all dogs as aggressive.

Overall, schemas are an important part of how we process and make sense of the world around us, but it is important to be aware of the potential for bias and to strive to update our schemas with accurate and complete information.

How are Schemas Created and Used as a Bias?

Schemas are created and used as a bias in several ways.

Schemas are often based on our past experiences and observations. If we have had mostly positive experiences with a certain group of people, we may have a schema that is biased in favour of that group. On the other hand, if we have had mostly negative experiences with a certain group, we may have a schema that is biased against that group.

Schemas can also be influenced by the media and other cultural influences. If we are exposed to media that portrays certain groups negatively or stereotypically, we may develop biased schemas about those groups.

People can also influence the schemas around us. If the people we interact with have biased views and beliefs, we may internalize those views and incorporate them into our schemas.

Schemas can be used as a bias in decision-making and problem-solving. If we have a biased schema about a certain group, we may be more likely to make decisions or solve problems in a way that is biased against that group.

Here are a few examples of gender-based schemas that may exist around us:

- **Stereotyped gender roles**: Some people may have a schema that associates certain activities, behaviours, or job functions with males or females. For example, they may believe that men are more suited to leadership roles, while women are more suited to support roles.
- **Gender stereotypes**: Some people may have a schema that associates certain characteristics or qualities with males or females. For example, they may believe that men are more logical and analytical, while women are more emotional and intuitive.
- **Gender-based expectations**: Some people may have a schema that associates certain behaviours or outcomes with males or females. For example, they may expect men to be more aggressive and assertive in the workplace, while they expect women to be more cooperative and nurturing
- **Gender biases in media and entertainment**: Some people may have a schema that is influenced by media and entertainment that reinforces gender stereotypes or portrays people of certain genders negatively or stereotypically.
- **Gender biases in education**: Some people may have a schema that is influenced by educational materials or practices that reinforce gender stereotypes or biases.

- **Gender biases in the home**: Some people may have a schema that is influenced by gender biases in their home environment.

It is important for individuals to be aware of the potential for gender-based schemas in the workplace and to strive to update their schemas with accurate and complete information. This can help to reduce the impact of gender bias in the workplace.

Overall, it is important to be aware of the potential for bias in our schemas and to strive to update them with accurate and complete information. This can help us to reduce the impact of bias in our thinking and decision-making.

Gender roles have changed so much over time, but we still operate from the past beliefs that were fed into us more than 30-40 years ago. It is time for us to upgrade ourselves to remain relevant. Let us now understand the impact that these unconscious beliefs create in our relationships at work.

I am certain that you would have found this journeying through our childhood beliefs and assessing that many of these beliefs may not be true would have opened a whole new way for you- the way you look at the world around you.

CHAPTER FOUR

Managing Bias at the Workplace

In today's diverse workplace, it is crucial to recognize and address the issue of bias. Bias can be defined as an inclination or prejudice for or against someone or something, and it can be conscious or unconscious. Bias can result in unfair treatment of individuals or groups, and it can create a toxic work environment that hinders productivity and innovation.

Managing bias in the workplace is a complex and ongoing process. It requires an understanding of the different forms of bias, their impact on individuals and the organization, and strategies to mitigate and eliminate them.

This book is designed to provide guidance on how to manage bias in the workplace. The chapter will highlight the importance of managing bias in the workplace, not only from an ethical and moral standpoint but also from a business perspective. A workplace that is free from bias fosters a culture of respect, inclusion, and collaboration, which can lead to improved employee engagement, productivity, and innovation. Understanding and addressing unconscious bias is critical to creating a truly inclusive workplace.

Managing bias in the workplace is a critical issue that requires ongoing attention and effort. This book aims to provide readers with a comprehensive understanding of the issue of bias, its impact, and strategies to mitigate and eliminate it. By creating a workplace that is free from bias, organizations can create a culture of inclusion and diversity that benefits everyone.

While explicit bias is easier to manage in the workplace, provided there are guidelines defined in the policies and procedures, implicit bias is difficult to be uprooted. Even though most organizations are aware there is a need for us to uproot the bias from organizational culture, it is still very difficult to implement this in letter and spirit.

Here are ten reasons why it may be difficult to eliminate implicit bias:

- Implicit biases are often unconscious and automatic, making them difficult to identify and control.
- Implicit biases are often deeply ingrained and may be based on past experiences and exposure to biased information.
- Implicit biases may be reinforced by the media and other cultural influences.
- Implicit biases may be reinforced by social norms and expectations.
- It may be difficult to challenge and change long-held beliefs and attitudes.
- It may be difficult to recognize and acknowledge one's own biases.
- It may be difficult to overcome the influence of biased information that has been internalized over time.
- It may be difficult to change behaviours that are based on implicit biases.

- It may be difficult to address the structural and systemic factors that contribute to implicit bias.
- It may be difficult to create a supportive environment that promotes unbiased thinking and behaviour.

Overall, eliminating implicit biases requires ongoing effort and a commitment to addressing and challenging biases at the individual, group, and societal levels.

Becoming aware of our personal biases is an important step in reducing their impact on our thinking, decision-making, and behaviour.

Here are a few ways to become more aware of our biases:

- **Reflect on your own experiences and beliefs:** Consider your own experiences and beliefs and how they may have shaped your biases. For example, think about your family, culture, and community and how they may have influenced your views.
- **Seek out diverse perspectives:** Expose yourself to diverse perspectives by reading and engaging with people who have different backgrounds, experiences, and viewpoints than you. This can help to broaden your perspective and challenge your biases.
- **Be open to new information:** Be open to new information and be willing to challenge your own assumptions and beliefs. Be open to the possibility that you may be wrong or that your views may change based on new information.
- **Be aware of your emotions:** Pay attention to your emotional reactions to certain people, ideas, or situations. These reactions may be a sign of an unconscious bias.

- **Seek feedback:** Ask for feedback from others about your behaviour and attitudes. This can help you to identify biases that you may not be aware of.
- **Take an Implicit Association Test (IAT):** The IAT is a psychological test that is designed to measure unconscious biases. Taking an IAT can help you to become more aware of your own biases and to identify areas where you may need to work on reducing your biases.

Overall, becoming aware of our personal biases requires self-reflection and a willingness to challenge our own assumptions and beliefs. It is an ongoing process that requires ongoing effort.

How do we as leaders and managers assist in 'interrupting' unconscious bias in the workplace?

Here are a few ways to interrupt unconscious bias in the workplace:

Overall, interrupting unconscious bias in the workplace requires a combination of self-awareness, education, and a commitment to inclusive and equitable behaviours and practices.

- **Educate Self:** Educate yourself and others about unconscious bias: Understanding what unconscious bias is and how it can impact decision-making, and behaviour is an important first step in interrupting it. Seek out resources and training on unconscious bias and share this information with your colleagues.
- **Be aware of your own biases:** Pay attention to your thoughts and actions and be aware of the potential for bias in your decision-making and behaviour. Reflect on your own experiences and beliefs and how they may be

influencing your biases.

- **Challenge Assumptions & Beliefs**: Be open to new information and perspectives and be willing to challenge your own assumptions and beliefs. Seek out diverse perspectives and be open to the possibility that your views may change based on new information.
- **Seek Feedback**: Ask for feedback from others about your behaviour and attitudes. This can help you to identify biases that you may not be aware of.
- **Avoid Labelling**: Avoid stereotyping and labelling people based on your assumptions, beliefs, and schemas. Remind yourself that most of these are based on your personal association and biases and are not universal truths.
- **Use inclusive language and behaviours:** Use language and behaviours that are inclusive of people of all genders, races, and backgrounds. Avoid making assumptions about people based on their appearance or stereotypes.
- **Become a Role Model**: Role of Leaders and Managers in interrupting bias at the workplace. In today's diverse and complex workplaces, leaders and managers play a crucial role in creating an inclusive and equitable environment. One key way in which they can do this is by interrupting bias and promoting diversity, equity, and inclusion (DEI) through their own behaviour and actions. By serving as positive role models, leaders and managers can help to set the tone for the workplace culture and demonstrate the values and behaviours that are expected of all employees. In this way, they can foster a workplace that is welcoming, respectful, and supportive of all individuals, regardless of their background or identity.

This chapter will explore the role of leaders and managers in interrupting bias in the workplace and the importance of role modelling in promoting DEI.

Let us dive deeper into finding a few simple ways in whichleaders and managers in interrupting bias in the workplace:

- **Set a positive example:** Leaders can help to interrupt conscious bias by setting a positive example for others to follow. This may involve using inclusive language and behaviours and actively promoting diversity and inclusion in the workplace.
- **Communicate expectations:** Leaders can help to interrupt conscious bias by clearly communicating expectations for behaviour and language that are inclusive and respectful. This may involve setting policies and guidelines that promote inclusivity and addressing instances of biased behaviour when they occur.
- **Educate self and others:** Leaders can help to interrupt conscious bias by educating themselves and others about unconscious bias and its impact on decision-making and behaviour. This may involve providing training and resources to support diversity and inclusion.
- **Foster a culture of inclusivity:** Leaders can help to interrupt conscious bias by fostering a culture of inclusivity and equity in the workplace. This may involve establishing diversity and inclusion goals and initiatives and creating opportunities for people of all genders, races, and backgrounds to be heard and valued.

Overall, leaders play a key role in interrupting conscious bias at the workplace by setting a positive example, communicating expectations, educating themselves and others, and fostering a culture of inclusivity and equity.

Become an Ally:

Another way by which managers and leaders can helping interrupting workplace bias is by acting as an ally. Allyship is a term that refers to an individual's commitment to supporting and advocating for marginalized groups. In the context of unconscious bias at the workplace, allyship can play an important role in interrupting conscious bias.

Here are a few ways that allyship can help to interrupt conscious bias in the workplace:

- **Challenging biased behaviours and language:** Allies can help to interrupt conscious bias by speaking up and challenging biased behaviour and language when they see it. This may involve calling out inappropriate comments or jokes or advocating for policies and practices that are inclusive and equitable.
- **Amplifying the voices of marginalized groups:** Allies can help to interrupt conscious bias by amplifying the voices and perspectives of marginalized groups. This may involve providing opportunities for these groups to speak or lead or support their ideas and initiatives.
- **Educating themselves and others about unconscious bias:** Allies can help to interrupt conscious bias by educating themselves and others about unconscious bias and its impact on decision-making and behaviour.
- **Modelling inclusive behaviour:** Allies can help to interrupt conscious bias by modelling inclusive behaviour and language, and by creating a safe and welcoming environment for people of all genders, races,

and backgrounds.

Overall, allyship plays an important role in interrupting conscious bias in the workplace by promoting inclusivity and equity, and by supporting and advocating for marginalized groups.

Reward Bystander Intervention:

Bystander intervention is a strategy that involves taking action to interrupt biased behaviour or language when it is witnessed. Bystander intervention can be an effective way to interrupt bias at the workplace, as it can help to create a culture of inclusivity and respect and to address instances of bias when they occur.

Here are a few strategies for bystander intervention at the workplace:

- **Speak up:** If you witness biased behaviour or language, consider speaking up and addressing it directly. You can do this in a respectful and non-confrontational way and use it as an opportunity to educate and raise awareness about the impact of bias.
- **Seek support:** If you feel uncomfortable or uncertain about how to intervene, consider seeking support from a colleague, supervisor, or HR representative.
- **Use inclusive language and behaviours**: Use inclusive language and behaviours in your interactions and encourage others to do the same.
- **Educate yourself and others**: Educate yourself and others about unconscious bias and its impact on decision-making and behaviour. This can help to create a culture of inclusivity and respect.

Overall, bystander intervention is an important strategy for interrupting bias in the workplace. By speaking up, seeking support, using inclusive language and behaviours, and educating ourselves and others, we can create a more inclusive and respectful work environment.

Question the Automatic Assumptions:

One way to question our automatic assumptions is to actively seek out and consider alternative perspectives. This can help us to challenge our own biases and see situations from different points of view.

It can also be helpful to seek out diverse sources of information, as this can expose us to a range of viewpoints that we may not have considered otherwise.

Additionally, it can be helpful to engage in reflective practices, such as journaling or discussing our thoughts and assumptions with others, as this can help us to identify and examine our biases more closely.

Finally, it can be helpful to educate ourselves about bias and how it can manifest in our thoughts and actions, as this can help us to become more aware of our biases and take steps to mitigate their impact.

Challenge the Microaggression:

A microaggression is a subtle but offensive comment or action directed at a minority or marginalized group. It can take many forms, such as racial slurs, derogatory comments about someone's gender or sexual orientation, or even something as seemingly innocent as asking someone where they are from or what they do for a living in a way that assumes they are not from the majority group or that they cannot be successful.

Microaggressions can be unintentional, but they can still hurt the person who experiences them and contribute to a harmful or hostile work environment. In the context of diversity and inclusion at the workplace, microaggressions can undermine efforts to create a more inclusive and welcoming environment for all employees.

Microaggressions act like an antagonist to the culture of inclusion and diversity. Microaggressions must be challenged to encourage a workplace culture that values diversity and promotes inclusivity. This may involve establishing diversity and inclusion goals and initiatives and providing training and resources to support diversity and inclusion.

Microaggressions can take the following forms amongst others:

- **Racial microaggressions:** These can include comments or actions that convey a belief that someone is not as intelligent or capable because of their race, such as being asked to speak on behalf of all people of a certain race or being told that they "speak good English."
- **Gender-related microaggressions:** These can include comments or actions that reinforce gender stereotypes or that imply that someone's gender makes them less qualified or capable, such as being called "sweetie" or "honey" by a co-worker or being passed over for a promotion because of assumptions about what kinds of work are suitable for someone of a certain gender. Another example could be a woman who may require leaving a bit early to pick up the child from the nearby daycare before boarding the office bus or drop service.
- **Sexual orientation-related microaggressions:** These can include comments or actions that convey a belief that someone's sexual orientation is abnormal or that they are not welcome because of their sexual orientation, such as using derogatory terms to describe

someone's sexual orientation or refusing to use someone's preferred pronouns.

- **Age-related microaggressions**: These can include comments or actions that convey a belief that someone is too old or too young to be competent or relevant, such as making jokes about someone's age or assuming that someone is not technologically savvy because of their age.
- **Disability-related microaggressions**: These can include comments or actions that convey a belief that someone is not as capable because of a disability, such as assuming that someone with a disability needs help when they do not ask for it or using derogatory language to describe someone's disability.

It is important not to underestimate the role of microaggressions and their potentially damaging impact on the workplace. People who suffer from microaggressions and don't complain are at the highest risk of cold quitting the organization.

Getting into the DEI Groove: Mindful inclusion (THINK Method):

Mindful inclusion is the practice of actively and intentionally creating an inclusive environment, where all individuals are valued, respected, and able to fully participate and contribute.

It involves being aware of and addressing power imbalances and biases that can prevent full inclusion and belonging, and creating opportunities for all individuals to have a sense of belonging and feel seen, heard, and valued.

This can involve things like actively seeking out diverse perspectives and voices, creating opportunities for dialogue and open communication, and intentionally considering inclusivity in decision-making processes.

Here are some benefits of using mindful inclusion and associated tools:

- **It involves self-awareness:** Being mindful of inclusion involves being aware of our own biases, assumptions, and privileges, as well as how these may impact our interactions and decisions. It also involves being open to learning and growing and being willing to listen to and consider the perspectives of others.
- **It requires active effort and continuous learning:** Mindful inclusion is not something that happens automatically – it requires conscious effort and intention. This may involve taking steps to create a more inclusive culture, such as setting clear expectations for behaviour, providing training on inclusivity, and actively seeking out and valuing diverse perspectives.
- **It creates a sense of belonging:** A key aspect of mindful inclusion is creating an environment where all individuals feel a sense of belonging and can fully participate. This can involve things like making sure that all voices are heard and that everyone feels comfortable speaking up, providing accommodations for individuals with disabilities, and being inclusive in language and communication.
- **It benefits everyone:** Creating a mindful and inclusive environment benefits everyone, not just those who have historically been marginalized or excluded. It allows all individuals to bring their full selves to work or school and can lead to increased creativity, productivity, and overall well-being.
- **It promotes self-reflection and personal development:** The THINK method encourages individuals to pause

and reflect on the potential impact of their words and actions before they speak or act. This can help individuals to be more mindful and considerate in their interactions with others, and to be more aware of how their words and actions might be perceived by others.

- **It can be used in various situations:** The THINK method can be applied in a wide range of situations, including in meetings when giving feedback when communicating with colleagues or clients, and in other interactions.
- **It can help to prevent misunderstandings or conflicts:** By using the THINK method, individuals can be more mindful of the potential impact of their words and actions and can take steps to avoid misunderstandings or conflicts that may arise due to a lack of awareness or consideration.

It can be used as part of a larger effort to build an inclusive culture.

The THINK method is just one tool that can be used as part of a larger effort to build a mindful and inclusive culture in the workplace. Other strategies may include providing training on inclusivity and diversity, setting clear expectations for behaviour, and actively seeking out and valuing diverse perspectives.

The THINK method is a tool that can be used to help individuals consider the potential impact of their words or actions on others. It can be a useful tool for building mindful inclusion in the workplace, as it can help individuals to be more aware of how their actions might be perceived by others and to take a more inclusive approach.

Using the THINK method can help individuals to be more mindful and considerate in their interactions with others, which can contribute to creating a more inclusive and positive workplace culture.

The THINK Method is a tool that can be used to challenge assumptions and avoid bias. It involves considering the following five questions:

Is it True?

Is the assumption that you are making supported by evidence, or is it based on incomplete or inaccurate information?

Before saying or doing something, consider whether it is based on fact and whether it is accurate.

Is it Helpful?

Does making this assumption help you to achieve your goals, or does it hinder your progress?

Think about whether what you are about to say or do will be helpful or constructive, or whether it might be harmful or divisive.

Is it Inspiring?

Does making this assumption motivate you to act, or does it discourage you?

Consider whether your words or actions will be inspiring or motivating to others, or whether they might discourage or demotivate.

Is it Necessary?

Is it necessary to make this assumption to reach a conclusion or decide, or is there another way to proceed?

Ask yourself whether what you are about to say or do is necessary or important, or whether it might be better left unsaid or undone.

Is it Kind?

Does making this assumption respect the rights and feelings of others, or does it hurt or discriminate against anyone?

Think about whether your words or actions will be kind and respectful to others, or whether they might be hurtful or unkind.

By asking yourself these questions, you can help to identify and challenge any assumptions that may be biased or not helpful and make more informed and unbiased decisions.

In our day-to-day experiences, we have seen how much implicit and unconscious bias still prevails in our work relationships and also in our family dynamics. Now that we have gained a deeper insight into how biases play at work, more so unconsciously or implicitly, in the subsequent chapters, let us understand what we can do now to promote a safe space at work, within our teams and departments that can foster a sense of belonging and create a culture where our people can bring their whole, authentic self to work so that they can deliver their best.

Here is an exercise that managers can use as the THINK method to challenge their own microaggressions:

- **Take notice:** Start by paying attention to your thoughts, feelings, and actions when interacting with colleagues and employees. Whenever you notice yourself having a thought or making a comment that could be perceived as a microaggression, pause and take note of it. Ask yourself: What was the microaggression? What triggered it? How did the other person respond?
- **Have empathy**: Put yourself in the shoes of the person who may have been impacted by the microaggression. Imagine how they might feel and how it could impact their sense of belonging and inclusion in the workplace. Ask yourself: How would I feel if I were in their position? What might be the consequences of my

microaggression for their well-being and productivity?

- **Investigate:** Take the time to investigate the underlying beliefs and assumptions that led to the microaggression. Ask yourself: What beliefs do I hold about this person or group of people that might have led to this microaggression? Where did these beliefs come from? Are they based on stereotypes or assumptions?

- **Neutralize:** Once you've identified the underlying beliefs and assumptions, work to neutralize them. Challenge your own biases and assumptions by seeking out information and perspectives that challenge your own worldview. Ask yourself: What evidence exists that contradicts my beliefs? How might my biases be impacting my behavior and interactions with others in the workplace?

- **Know better:** Commit to doing better by educating yourself on issues related to diversity, equity, and inclusion in the workplace. Seek out resources and training opportunities that can help you become a more effective and inclusive leader. Ask yourself: How can I learn more about the experiences of people from different backgrounds? How can I build stronger relationships with colleagues and employees from diverse backgrounds?

By using the THINK method to challenge your own microaggressions, you can become a more effective and inclusive leader, creating a more positive and productive workplace for everyone. It's important to approach this work with an open mind and a willingness to be honest with yourself, even when it's uncomfortable. With time and practice, you can develop greater self-awareness and empathy, and become a stronger advocate for diversity, equity, and inclusion in the workplace.

CHAPTER FIVE

Uncovering the Unconscious Bias during Recruitment & Selection

Being conscious during the recruitment and selection process is important to avoid bias, as it can help to ensure that the best candidates are selected based on their qualifications and skills, rather than on factors such as their race, gender, age, or sexuality.

Bias during the recruitment and selection process can lead to a lack of diversity and representation among employees, which can have negative effects on both the employees and the company. For example, a lack of diversity can lead to a lack of different perspectives and ideas, which can negatively impact decision-making and problem-solving. It can also lead to a lack of understanding and connection with customers from different backgrounds, which can be especially detrimental for companies that operate in a global market.

Additionally, bias during the recruitment and selection process can also lead to discrimination, which is not only morally and ethically wrong, but also illegal in many countries. Discrimination can lead to a hostile work environment and low employee morale, which can lead to high turnover rates and decreased productivity.

Being conscious during the recruitment and selection process can help to avoid bias by implementing fair and objective selection criteria, such as qualifications and skills, and by avoiding subjective criteria, such as race, gender, age, or sexuality. It can also include training on unconscious bias, and actively recruiting and promoting individuals from marginalized communities.

Additionally, involving a diverse group of people in the recruitment and selection process can also help to reduce bias and increase diversity and representation among employees.

While recruitment and selection processes are most subjected to conscious and unconscious biases, being conscious during the recruitment and selection process is important to avoid bias, ensure diversity, representation, and fair opportunities, and create a positive and productive work environment.

Here are a few ways to uncover the unconscious bias in recruitment & selection:

- **Be Mindful of your Job Titles:** Sometimes we inadvertently mention, 'hiring a salesman, reporting to the chairman.' This would be better off using more inclusive language such as, 'hiring a salesperson (not salesman) who will report to the Chairperson (not the Chairman) in the title.

- **Check for Gender Bias:**Avoid words such as "aggressively" which may be perceived as masculine in each job description. Use of everyday words such as 'guys', 'workmanship', and 'godfather', which represent a particular segment must be avoided. Use words like 'partners' instead of 'spouse or wives'.
- **Be Wary of the LGBTQ Unconscious Bias ("Personal Pronouns"):** It used to be that you covered both your bases if you used "he/she" and "his/her" language like the job description below. No more. Now, if you want to be inclusive, you are best off using "they/their" language.
- **Be Mindful of the "Maternity" Bias:** More progressive/ modern companies are using alternative words and phrases for "maternity" such as Parental time off.
- **Be Careful with Disability Related Bias:** There are numerous words used in everyday language that turn off someone with (or close to someone with) a disability.

  - "speak" ("communicate" is better)
  - "see" ("identify," "assess" and "discover" are better)
  - "carry" ("move" is better)
  - "walk" ("traverse" is better)

- **Be aware of the Age-Related Bias:** Words like "young" is problematic. So is "digital native" as it suggests you only want to hire someone who is grown up in the computer/Internet age. Instead, try spelling out the skills you need ("familiarity with video games" is better than "digital native"). Similarly, if your job ad mentions wanting a "recent college grad" or needing someone "young and energetic," you could get into a lawsuit, especially if working in a country with stricter laws.

Keeping the above in mind, here are the top ten, easy to do strategies for minimizing bias in recruitment and selection:

- **Use objective criteria to evaluate candidates:** This means relying on qualifications and skills that are relevant to the job, rather than subjective qualities like appearance or demeanour. This can include things like education, work experience, and specific skills and abilities.
- **Use structured interviews:** Structured interviews involve asking all candidates the same set of standardized questions, which can help to reduce bias by ensuring that all candidates are evaluated consistently. Structured interviews are an effective way to reduce D&I related bias during recruitment by ensuring that all candidates are assessed using a consistent set of criteria. Here's the process for using structured interviews:

Identify the job requirements: Before the interview process begins, identify the specific skills, knowledge, and experience required for the job. This will help you create a set of objective criteria for assessing candidates.

Develop a set of standardized questions: Develop a set of questions that are based on the job requirements and that are asked of all candidates. This helps ensure that all candidates are evaluated using the same criteria.

Train interviewers: Train all interviewers on the interview process and the use of standardized questions. Emphasize the importance of reducing bias and provide guidance on how to do so.

Use a diverse interview panel: Include a diverse set of interviewers on the panel to reduce the potential for bias. This can include individuals from different backgrounds, genders, races, and cultures.

Provide a grievance redressal mechanism: Make sure to provide a mechanism for candidates to file complaints about any unfair treatment or discrimination they may experience during the interview process. Communicate this mechanism to all candidates in advance.

Use a scoring rubric: Develop a scoring rubric that aligns with the job requirements and the standardized questions. This helps ensure that all candidates are evaluated consistently and objectively.

Conduct the interviews: During the interview, ask each candidate the same set of standardized questions and use the scoring rubric to evaluate their responses. Avoid asking illegal or inappropriate questions (as mentioned in my previous response) and focus on the candidate's qualifications, experience, and fit for the job.

Evaluate the results: After all interviews are completed, evaluate the results using the scoring rubric. This helps ensure that all candidates are evaluated consistently and objectively.

By including a diverse interview panel and providing a grievance redressal mechanism, you can further reduce D&I related bias during recruitment. Remember to communicate the mechanism to all candidates in advance and provide a way for them to file complaints if needed. This can help promote a fair and inclusive hiring process for all candidates.

- **Avoid asking illegal or inappropriate questions:** It is illegal to ask candidates about certain protected characteristics, such as their race, religion, age, or marital status. Avoiding these types of questions can help to prevent any potential legal issues.

It's important for employers to be aware of the questions that are illegal or inappropriate to ask during interviews, both in India and globally, to avoid discrimination and promote a fair and inclusive hiring process. Here are some examples of questions that should not be asked during interviews:

Age: It is illegal to ask candidates about their age, as this can lead to age discrimination. Instead, focus on the candidate's qualifications and experience.

Marital status: Questions about a candidate's marital status, such as whether they are married or planning to have children, are inappropriate and can lead to gender discrimination.

Religion: It is illegal to ask candidates about their religion, as this can lead to religious discrimination. Focus on the candidate's qualifications and experience instead.

Disability: Questions about a candidate's disability or medical history are inappropriate and can lead to disability discrimination. Focus on the candidate's ability to perform the job duties.

Sexual orientation: It is illegal to ask candidates about their sexual orientation, as this can lead to discrimination based on sexual orientation.

National origin: Questions about a candidate's national origin, such as their place of birth or ethnicity, are inappropriate and can lead to discrimination based on race or ethnicity.

Salary history: Asking about a candidate's current or previous salary history can perpetuate pay inequity and should be avoided. Instead, focus on the candidate's desired salary range.

By avoiding these illegal or inappropriate questions during interviews, employers can promote a fair and inclusive hiring process and reduce the risk of discrimination. It's important for employers to educate themselves and their hiring managers on what questions are appropriate and what questions should be avoided during interviews.

- **Consider using diverse recruitment sources:** Relying on the same recruitment sources can lead to a lack of diversity in your candidate pool. Consider using a variety of sources, such as job fairs, networking events, and online job boards, to attract a more diverse group of candidates.

To avoid D&I related bias in recruitment, it's important to use diverse recruitment sources that are inclusive and representative of different backgrounds and communities. Here are some examples of such sources:

Social media platforms: LinkedIn, Facebook, and Twitter are great social media platforms to connect with potential candidates from diverse backgrounds. By using specific hashtags and targeted advertising, recruiters can reach out to candidates from different communities.

Job boards and career fairs: Job boards such as Naukri, Indeed, and Monster are popular platforms to advertise job openings and reach a diverse pool of candidates. Career fairs such as the Women in Technology (WIT) conference and the National Career Service Job Fair provide opportunities to meet and engage with a diverse group of job seekers.

Employee referrals: Employee referrals are a great way to source diverse candidates. Encouraging existing employees to refer candidates from different communities can help build a more diverse workforce.

Professional associations and affinity groups: Professional associations such as the Society for Human Resource Management (SHRM) and the National Association of Software and Services Companies (NASSCOM) provide opportunities to connect with candidates from specific communities and backgrounds. Affinity groups such as the LGBTQIA+ employee resource group or the Women's network can also be a great source of diverse talent.

Non-profit organizations: Non-profit organizations such as Teach For India, Make a Difference, and CRY work with specific communities and groups and can be a great source for diverse candidates.

Diversity-focused recruitment agencies: Diversity-focused recruitment agencies such as Vercida Consulting, PurpleStride, and Diversity Solutions can help source and hire candidates from diverse backgrounds and communities. These agencies specialize in diversity and inclusion and can provide guidance on creating an inclusive recruitment process.

By using these diverse recruitment sources, you can create a more inclusive and representative candidate pool, helping to reduce D&I related bias in the hiring process. Remember to be intentional about reaching out to candidates from different backgrounds and communities and to be mindful of unconscious biases that may impact the recruitment process.

- **Use software to screen resumes:** Resume screening software can help to eliminate bias by removing personal information from resumes, such as names and addresses. This can help to ensure that candidates are evaluated based on their qualifications and skills rather than their personal characteristics.

There are several resume screening software available in India that can help avoid D&I related biases. Here are a few examples:

Talview: Talview is an AI-powered recruitment software that uses natural language processing (NLP) to analyze resumes and identify any biases that may be present. It also includes features like blind hiring and skill-based assessments to help eliminate biases in the recruitment process.

Skillate: Skillate is an AI-driven recruitment automation software that uses machine learning algorithms to screen resumes and identify the best-fit candidates for a job. It includes features like anonymization and gender-neutral language to help reduce bias in the hiring process.

Entelo: Entelo is a recruiting automation platform that includes features like diversity insights, which provides recruiters with data on the gender and ethnic diversity of their candidate pool. It also includes a feature called Entelo Diversity, which helps identify and source candidates from underrepresented groups.

Shortlist: Shortlist is a recruiting software that includes features like candidate matching and screening, which helps eliminate unconscious bias by identifying candidates based on their skills and qualifications, rather than demographic factors.

It's important to note that while these tools can be helpful in identifying and reducing bias in the recruitment process, they should not be relied on exclusively. It's still important for recruiters and hiring managers to undergo training and education on diversity, equity, and inclusion to ensure that they are making informed and unbiased hiring decisions.

- **Involve diverse team members in the selection process:** Having a diverse group of people involved in the selection process can help to reduce bias by providing different perspectives and experiences.

Involving diverse team members in the selection process is an effective way to reduce bias and promote a more inclusive hiring process. Here are some steps you can take to involve diverse team members in the selection process:

Define the selection criteria: Before involving team members in the selection process, define the selection criteria for the role. This will ensure that all team members are evaluating candidates based on the same criteria.

Select the team members: Select team members from different backgrounds, genders, races, and cultures to participate in the selection process. This will help reduce bias and ensure that diverse perspectives are represented.

Train the team members: Provide training to team members on the selection criteria, the interview process, and how to evaluate candidates objectively. This will help ensure that all team members are evaluating candidates fairly and consistently.

Assign specific roles: Assign specific roles to each team member during the selection process. For example, one team member can conduct initial screening interviews, while another can evaluate the candidates' technical skills.

Facilitate communication: Encourage team members to share their opinions and feedback during the selection process. This can be done through regular check-ins or debrief meetings after each interview round.

Evaluate the results: After all interviews are completed, evaluate the results as a team. This will ensure that all team members have a say in the final decision and that diverse perspectives are taken into account.

Involving diverse team members in the selection process is a valuable way to reduce bias and promote a more inclusive hiring process. By following these steps, you can ensure that all team members are evaluating candidates fairly and consistently based on the selection criteria.

When assembling a diverse interview panel, it's important to consider a range of backgrounds, experiences, and perspectives. Here are three examples of diverse teams that could be used to conduct an interview panel:

Gender-diverse team: A gender-diverse team includes individuals from different genders, such as male, female, and non-binary. This team can bring diverse perspectives on workplace culture, communication, and collaboration. Additionally, having a gender-diverse team can help reduce the potential for gender bias during the selection process.

Culturally diverse team: A culturally diverse team includes individuals from different ethnicities and cultural backgrounds. This team can bring diverse perspectives on communication styles, teamwork, and problem-solving. Additionally, having a culturally diverse team can help reduce the potential for cultural bias during the selection process.

Skill-diverse team: A skill-diverse team includes individuals with different skills, experience, and backgrounds related to the job requirements. This team can bring diverse perspectives on the technical aspects of the role, as well as the soft skills needed for success in the position. Additionally, having a skill-diverse team can help ensure that all candidates are evaluated fairly and objectively based on the job requirements.

It's important to remember that these are just a few examples of diverse teams that could be used to conduct an interview panel. Depending on the job requirements and the candidate pool, there may be other factors to consider when assembling a diverse team. The key is to consider a range of backgrounds and perspectives to ensure a fair and inclusive hiring process.

- **Offer equal opportunities for remuneration and advancement**: Ensuring that all employees have equal opportunities for advancement can help to reduce bias and create a more diverse and inclusive workplace. This can include things like training and development programs, mentorship opportunities, and clear career advancement paths.

There have been several cases in India where companies have been sued for not offering equal opportunities for remuneration and advancement to their employees, including cases of gender-based discrimination.

One such case is the lawsuit filed against Hindustan Electro Graphites (HEG) by a group of female employees who alleged that the company was not offering equal opportunities for remuneration and advancement based on gender. The lawsuit alleged that the company had a discriminatory policy that favored male employees in terms of promotions and salary hikes. The case was filed in the Delhi High Court, and the court issued notices to the company and the Ministry of Women and Child Development to respond to the allegations.

The case is an example of how discrimination based on gender can lead to legal action in India. It also highlights the importance of ensuring equal opportunities for remuneration and advancement to all employees, regardless of gender, race, religion, or any other protected characteristic.

In 2021, a transwoman candidate filed a lawsuit against a public sector undertaking (PSU) alleging discrimination during the recruitment process. The candidate alleged that she was denied employment because of her gender identity, despite fulfilling all the eligibility criteria.

In 2019, a woman candidate filed a lawsuit against a private company alleging discrimination during the recruitment process. The candidate alleged that she was rejected for a job because she was pregnant, despite being highly qualified and experienced for the position.

In 2018, a PwD candidate filed a lawsuit against a multinational company alleging discrimination during the recruitment process. The candidate alleged that she was not given a fair opportunity to compete for a job because the company did not provide appropriate accommodations for her disability during the selection process.

These lawsuits highlight the need for employers to ensure a fair and inclusive recruitment process that does not discriminate against candidates based on their gender, disability status, or any other protected characteristic. Employers should make sure to provide equal opportunities for all candidates and ensure that the recruitment process is accessible to PwD candidates by providing necessary accommodations.

- **Provide diversity and inclusion training to hiring managers and recruiters**: Training can help to raise awareness of unconscious biases and how they can impact the recruitment and selection process. It can also provide tools and strategies for addressing and minimizing bias.

When providing diversity and inclusion training to hiring managers and recruiters, the content coverage should include:

Understanding diversity and inclusion: The training should cover the basics of diversity and inclusion, including the importance of creating a diverse and inclusive workplace, the benefits of diversity, and the impact of bias on recruitment and selection.

Identifying biases: The training should help managers and recruiters identify their own biases and how they can influence recruitment decisions. It should also provide tools and strategies to reduce the impact of unconscious bias on the recruitment process.

Legal considerations: The training should cover the legal requirements and implications of discrimination and bias in recruitment and selection, including the various laws and regulations that protect against discrimination in India.

Best practices for inclusive recruitment: The training should provide practical guidance on how to make the recruitment process more inclusive, including strategies for reaching out to diverse candidate pools, using inclusive language in job postings, and creating an interview process that is fair and unbiased.

Communication and feedback: The training should cover how to communicate with candidates from diverse backgrounds and how to provide feedback that is respectful and constructive, regardless of whether or not the candidate is selected for the position.

Ongoing learning and development: The training should emphasize the importance of ongoing learning and development in creating a diverse and inclusive workplace, and provide resources and opportunities for managers and recruiters to continue their education and development in this area.

Overall, the training should be comprehensive and designed to provide hiring managers and recruiters with the knowledge, skills, and tools they need to ensure that the recruitment process is fair, inclusive, and free from bias and discrimination.

- **Use blind resumes:** Removing personal information from resumes, such as names and addresses, can help to reduce bias during the resume review process. This can help to ensure that candidates are evaluated based on their qualifications and skills rather than their personal characteristics.

  Using a blind resume is a process of removing any identifying information such as name, gender, age, ethnicity, and address from a candidate's resume to avoid D&I-related unconscious bias during the recruitment process. Here's how the process can be implemented:

Identify the information to be removed: Determine the information that needs to be removed from the resumes. This may include name, gender, age, ethnicity, and address. Other personal information such as hobbies and interests should also be removed.

Create a standardized format: Develop a standardized format for resumes that removes identifying information while retaining the relevant job-related information. The format should be consistent across all resumes.

Implement the blind resume policy: Announce the blind resume policy to all recruiters and hiring managers. Ensure that they understand the reason for the policy and how it will be implemented.

Review resumes without identifying information: Review resumes without any identifying information, and assess the candidates based solely on their qualifications and experience.

Conduct interviews: Once the resumes have been reviewed, conduct interviews with the candidates who meet the required qualifications. During the interview process, ensure that all questions are job-related and free from any bias.

Uncover candidate identity: Once the interview process is complete, reveal the candidate identities and conduct any necessary background checks.

Using a blind resume is a simple yet effective way to reduce the impact of unconscious bias during the recruitment process. By removing identifying information from resumes, recruiters and hiring managers can focus on the candidate's qualifications and experience without any preconceived biases based on gender, ethnicity, age, or any other protected characteristic. It is important to note that while the blind resume process can reduce the impact of unconscious bias, it is not a substitute for a comprehensive diversity and inclusion strategy that addresses systemic issues and fosters an inclusive workplace culture.

- **Monitor and track your progress:** Set diversity hiring targets. Regularly tracking and monitoring the diversity of your candidate pool and hires can help to identify areas where bias may be present and allow you to take steps to address it. This can include collecting and analysing data on the diversity of your candidates and hires and setting diversity goals and targets.

To monitor and track progress in D&I related hiring and to avoid unconscious bias, organizations can use several matrices to measure their success. Here are some examples:

Applicant Pool Diversity: Measure the diversity of the applicant pool by tracking the number and percentage of applicants from different backgrounds, such as gender, ethnicity, age, and disability.

Interview Panel Diversity: Track the diversity of the interview panel by measuring the number and percentage of panel members from different backgrounds.

Offer and Acceptance Rates: Monitor the offer and acceptance rates for different groups to ensure that all candidates are given equal opportunities.

Time-to-Fill: Track the time-to-fill for different positions to identify any discrepancies in the recruitment process that may be causing delays or preventing certain groups from being hired.

Employee Retention: Monitor employee retention rates for different groups to ensure that all employees are treated fairly and provided with equal opportunities for growth and development.

Employee Satisfaction: Conduct regular employee satisfaction surveys to identify any issues related to diversity and inclusion in the workplace.

By tracking and monitoring these metrics, organizations can identify areas for improvement and make necessary changes to ensure a more diverse and inclusive hiring process. It's important to remember that D&I is an ongoing process, and progress should be regularly monitored and evaluated to ensure that organizations are creating a culture of equity and inclusion.

- **Crafting Inclusive Job descriptions**: Avoid Gender-Coded Words. Being mindful of your job description vocabulary can make a big difference. Studies show that gender-coded words can significantly reduce the number of women applying to your open positions, even though this type of bias is usually unconscious. To make your job descriptions more inclusive, start by taking gendered words like "ninja," rock star," or "guru" out of your job titles and replacing them with more straightforward titles, like "developer" or "sales representative." These titles may have less flair, but they are also more inclusive and less likely to turn off candidates who feel they do not fit the image you are putting out.Next, go through and remove any other gender-coded words that might pop up throughout your descriptions—for both men and women. Keep these words in mind when writing your job descriptions to make the language more appealing to all applicants. Certain tools can tell you right away whether your job ad leans too much towards either feminine or masculine-coded words.

Crafting inclusive job descriptions is an important step in creating a diverse and inclusive hiring process. Here are some steps to follow:

Remove gendered language: Start by removing gendered language from the job description. This includes using words like "he" or "she," and instead using gender-neutral language like "they" or "the candidate."

Avoid cultural references: Avoid using cultural references or idioms that may be unfamiliar to candidates from different backgrounds. This will help ensure that the job description is accessible to a wider pool of candidates.

Use neutral job titles: Use neutral job titles that accurately describe the role and responsibilities of the position, rather than using titles that may be biased towards a certain gender or demographic.

Emphasize company values: Emphasize the company's commitment to diversity and inclusion in the job description. This sends a clear message to candidates that the company is dedicated to creating a welcoming and inclusive workplace.

Use inclusive language: Use inclusive language throughout the job description to make all candidates feel welcome and valued. This includes avoiding terms that may be exclusive, such as "young" or "able-bodied."

Highlight flexibility: Highlight any flexibility or accommodations that the company can provide to candidates who may have different needs or requirements. This can include flexible work schedules, remote work options, or accommodations for disabilities.

Review and revise: Review the job description with a critical eye to identify any potential biases or language that may be exclusive. Revise the job description as needed to ensure that it is inclusive and welcoming to all candidates.

By following these steps, recruiters and hiring managers can create job descriptions that are inclusive and welcoming to all candidates, regardless of their background or identity. This can help to attract a diverse pool of candidates and promote a culture of diversity and inclusion in the workplace.

- **Limit your job requirements to 'must-haves'**: As a hiring manager, you may have an unending list of qualifications in mind for a given role, highlighting your commitment to inclusion, and it is important to trim the list down. That is because studies show that while men are likely to apply to jobs for which they meet only 60% of the qualifications, women are much more likely to hesitate unless they meet 100% of the listed requirements. Instead of including all the "nice-to-haves" that a dream candidate might possess, stick to the "must-haves," and you will see your applications from women candidates increase. Or if you would still like to call out certain desired skills, you can soften the message with language like "familiarity with," "bonus points for," or "if you have any combination of these skills." That said, it is a good idea to cut down your long list no matter what—one study found that the average job seeker spends just 49.7 seconds reviewing a listing before deciding it is not a fit. So, stick to the essentials.

When conducting an inclusive interview, it's important to limit your job requirements to 'must-haves' to avoid unconscious bias. Here are some steps to follow:

Define the essential job requirements: Start by defining the essential job requirements for the role. This includes skills, experience, and qualifications that are necessary to perform the job successfully.

Eliminate non-essential requirements: Review the job requirements and eliminate any that are non-essential to the job. This can include requirements that may be biased towards a certain demographic or that are not directly related to the job responsibilities.

Focus on the candidate's potential: Focus on the candidate's potential to learn and grow, rather than solely on their past experience or qualifications. This can help to identify candidates who may have transferable skills or who may be able to learn quickly on the job.

Avoid 'nice-to-have' requirements: Avoid including 'nice-to-have' requirements in the job description or interview process. These can create unnecessary barriers for candidates who may not meet these requirements, but who may still be qualified for the job.

Use structured interviews: Use a structured interview process that focuses on the essential job requirements. This can help to ensure that all candidates are evaluated based on the same criteria, and can reduce the impact of unconscious bias.

By limiting job requirements to 'must-haves' and focusing on the candidate's potential, recruiters and hiring managers can create a more inclusive interview process that is open to a wider range of candidates. This can help to attract a diverse pool of candidates and promote a culture of diversity and inclusion in the workplace.

- **Avoid using unnecessary corporate speech and jargon:** One of the quickest ways to turn off candidates is to include loads of unnecessary jargon in your descriptions. That includes things like KPIs, procurement, SLAs, P&L, and so on. While candidates with plenty of experience in a similar role might know what you are talking about, studies show jargon and corporate language in job postings are one of the biggest barriers keeping talented young people from applying to entry-level positions. These subtle word choices can make some candidates feel unqualified for a position for which they are qualified. For example, instead of using mystifying acronyms and sales terms in your requirements, aim for more universal wording that remains standard across industries.

    Using unnecessary corporate speech and jargon can create barriers and exclude candidates who may not be familiar with these terms. Here are some steps to avoid using unnecessary corporate speech and jargon:

    Use simple language: Use simple and clear language in your job descriptions and interviews. Avoid using complex terms and jargon that may not be familiar to everyone.

    Keep it concise: Keep your job descriptions and interviews concise and to the point. Avoid using long sentences or complicated language.

Use inclusive language: Use language that is inclusive and avoids bias. For example, avoid using gender-specific pronouns and use gender-neutral terms instead.

Test your language: Test your language with a diverse group of people to ensure that it is easily understandable and inclusive.

Focus on the job requirements: Focus on the essential job requirements and avoid using unnecessary language or jargon that may not be relevant to the job.

By using simple and clear language, focusing on the job requirements, and using inclusive language, recruiters and hiring managers can create a more inclusive job description and interview process that is accessible to a wider range of candidates. This can help to attract a more diverse pool of candidates and promote a culture of diversity and inclusion in the workplace.

- **Emphasize organizational commitment to diversity and inclusion:** Once you have a clear DEI Mission statement, a lot flows from there. Diversity and inclusion only work when you can take into consideration the organization that you have, the business that you are in, the culture that you have today, and the culture you want. So really think through those nuances and those crucial factors. It is the only way you can be successful. Employees are drawn to, work harder in, and simply care more about organizations that show they care about their people. Once you have achieved this, translate the DEI strategy into your Employee Value Proposition and use this for external branding in the targeted audience pool. If your company is already making major strides toward becoming a more welcoming and inclusive place to work, you might want to consider including this in your job descriptions. While you can simply state at the bottom that you are "an equality opportunity employer," a statement in your own words is more powerful. Online career pages that have a special disclaimer that the Company has zero tolerance for discrimination and does not discriminate based on caste, colour, creed, gender, sexual orientation, family background or marital status make a lot of difference in the way the prospective candidates perceive your organization. Here are some examples of a pitch to emphasize organizational commitment to diversity and inclusion:

- "At our company, we believe that diversity is a strength. We are committed to building a team that reflects the diversity of our customers and the communities we serve. We strive to create a workplace culture that values and respects all individuals, regardless of their background, gender, race, ethnicity, religion, or sexual orientation."
- "Diversity and inclusion are not just buzzwords at our company - they are core values that guide everything we do. We believe that our diversity is our strength and that by bringing together individuals with different backgrounds, experiences, and perspectives, we can drive innovation, creativity, and growth."
- "We recognize that creating a diverse and inclusive workplace requires more than just words - it requires action. That's why we have implemented a range of initiatives to attract, retain, and promote a diverse workforce, including unconscious bias training for our hiring managers, flexible work arrangements,

and mentoring programs."

  ○ "Our commitment to diversity and inclusion is not just a box to check - it's a business imperative. By creating a culture where everyone feels valued and included, we can unlock the full potential of our workforce and drive business success. We are proud to be a company that values diversity, equity, and inclusion, and we are committed to continuously improving in this area."

- **Call out inclusive benefits:** You already know that benefits like paid parental leave, childcare subsidies, paid family sick time, and even health insurance go a long way toward supporting diversity and inclusion, while also boosting retention and morale. If your company offers these benefits, you may not realize the need to call them out in job descriptions—since not every employee will necessarily benefit from them—but mentioning them allows you to prove your commitment to inclusion right away. You do not have to include every benefit but adding a few perks to your postings does not hurt. Your job posting is likely to be your first touch point with a candidate, and jobseekers with families (or who are looking to start families at some point) will see the benefits mentioned in your descriptions as signals of your larger company values. Because we all have biases that can be unconscious and unintentional, it is always a good idea to revisit your job descriptions and make tweaks to make them more inclusive and, if applicable, show off the great work your company is already doing to boost diversity and inclusion.

    Here are some examples of inclusive benefits offered by Indian organizations:

Tata Consultancy Services (TCS) - TCS offers a program called 'TCS iBegin' which is a hiring initiative for differently-abled individuals. It aims to provide job opportunities to people with visual, auditory, and orthopedic disabilities.

Accenture India - Accenture India offers a 'Pride Ally' program that provides support and resources to LGBTQ+ employees. The program aims to create a safe and inclusive workplace for all employees regardless of their sexual orientation or gender identity.

Infosys - Infosys offers a 'Women in Technology' program that aims to increase the number of women in technology roles. The program provides training, mentoring, and career development opportunities to women employees.

Godrej - Godrej has a program called 'Disha' which aims to provide employment opportunities to people with disabilities. The program offers training and development programs, customized workstations, and assistive devices to support employees with disabilities.

Wipro - Wipro offers a program called 'Autism at Work' which aims to provide job opportunities to individuals with autism. The program provides training and support to help individuals with autism succeed in the workplace.

By offering inclusive benefits and programs, these organizations are creating a more diverse and inclusive workplace. This not only benefits the employees but also helps the organization to attract and retain top talent.

- **Conduct Inclusive Interviews:** An inclusive interview is a recruitment process that is designed to be fair and unbiased, and that actively seeks to include and consider candidates from diverse backgrounds and experiences. An inclusive interview process can take many different forms, but it involves:

- A diverse group of interviewers to evaluate candidates. This can help to ensure that a wide range of perspectives is considered and that biases are minimized.
- Using structured, consistent interview processes and rating systems to ensure that all candidates are fairly evaluated. This might include using standardized interview questions and evaluating candidates based on specific criteria related to the job.
- Avoiding non-inclusive language or asking questions that could be interpreted as biased or discriminatory. This includes avoiding questions about candidates' age, marital status, nationality, or other personal characteristics that are not related to the job.
- Creating a welcoming space for all. Try to create a welcoming and inclusive environment for all candidates. This might include providing accommodations for candidates with disabilities or offering language translation services for non-native English speakers.
- Seeking input and feedback from diverse stakeholders, including employees and community members, to ensure the recruitment process is fair and representative.

- **Question what matters:** It is important to question what matters only in an inclusive interview to avoid unconscious bias because this helps to focus on the candidate's qualifications, skills, and experience rather than irrelevant personal characteristics such as gender, race, ethnicity, religion, or sexual orientation. By questioning only what is necessary, interviewers can ensure that they are evaluating candidates fairly and objectively, based on their ability to perform the job duties. This approach also helps to avoid assumptions or stereotypes that can lead to unconscious bias in the hiring process. Inclusive interviews that focus on the candidate's qualifications and skills can lead to a more diverse and inclusive workplace, where employees feel valued and respected for their contributions. This can improve employee engagement, productivity, and retention, and help to attract top talent from a wide range of backgrounds. Here are a few tips for asking the right questions during an inclusive interview process:

- Make sure that the questions you ask are related to the skills and competencies required for the job. Avoid asking questions that could be perceived as biased or discriminatory, such as questions about candidates' age, marital status, nationality, or other personal characteristics that are not related to the job.
- Use open-ended questions that allow candidates to provide examples of their skills and experience. This can help you to get a better sense of how candidates have demonstrated the competencies required for the role in the past.
- Avoid asking leading questions that suggest a specific answer or that could put candidates on the spot.
- Consider using behavioural interview questions, which ask candidates to provide specific examples

of how they have demonstrated certain skills or behaviours in the past. This can help you to better understand how candidates have applied their skills and experience in real-world situations. Here are a few examples of questions that should be avoided during an inclusive interview process:

- Questions about candidates' age, unless they are relevant to the job (e.g., "Are you over 18?")
- Questions about candidates' marital status, unless they are relevant to the job (e.g., "Are you married?", "When do you plan to get married?")
- Questions about candidates' religion, unless they are relevant to the job (e.g., "What church do you attend?")
- Questions about candidates' sexual orientation, unless they are relevant to the job (e.g., "Are you gay?")
- Questions about candidates' national origin or citizenship, unless they are relevant to the job (e.g., "Where were you born?")
- Questions about candidates' family status or responsibilities, unless they are relevant to the job (e.g., "Do you have children?")
- Questions about candidates' physical or mental disabilities, unless they are relevant to the job (e.g., "Do you have any physical disabilities?")
- Questions about candidates' caste or social status.
- Questions about candidates' native language or accent.
- Questions about candidates' family background or connections.

- Questions about candidates' physical appearance, such as their colour weight, or skin colour.
- Questions about candidates' personal relationships or family planning.
- Questions about candidates' political beliefs or affiliations.

- **Managing Bias for Referral Hiring**: Managing bias for referral hiring is important because referrals are a common source of new hires in many organizations, and relying solely on referrals can lead to a lack of diversity in the workforce. Referral hiring can perpetuate homogeneity in the workplace, as employees are more likely to refer people who are similar to themselves in terms of gender, race, ethnicity, education, and social background.

  To ensure that referral hiring is fair and inclusive, it is important to manage bias by implementing structured referral programs, setting clear guidelines and expectations for referrals, and actively seeking referrals from a diverse pool of sources. This can include encouraging referrals from employee resource groups, professional associations, community organizations, and social networks.

  By managing bias in referral hiring, organizations can increase the diversity of their workforce, which can lead to a range of benefits, including improved innovation, creativity, and problem-solving. A more diverse workforce can also better reflect the diversity of customers and clients, which can lead to better relationships and increased business opportunities.
  Here are a few tips for ensuring that bias is avoided when a leader refers a candidate:

- ◦ Develop clear criteria and guidelines for the referral process, and make sure that all employees, including leaders, are aware of these guidelines.
- ◦ Encourage leaders to refer a diverse pool of candidates. This might include providing diversity and inclusion training to help leaders understand the importance of diversity and how to identify potential candidates from underrepresented groups.
- ◦ Use structured, consistent interview processes and rating systems to ensure that all candidates are fairly evaluated. This might include using standardized interview questions and evaluating candidates based on specific criteria related to the job.
- ◦ Consider using "blind" resume review processes, in which identifying information such as names and addresses are removed from resumes before they are reviewed. This can help to reduce bias in the review process.
- ◦ Seek input and feedback from diverse stakeholders, including employees and community members, to ensure that the referral process is fair and representative.
- ◦ Regularly review and assess the effectiveness of the referral program and adjust as needed to ensure that it is inclusive and unbiased.

- **Have a Formal Appeal Process:** Having a formal appeal process is important in the context of D&I interviews to avoid unconscious bias because it provides a mechanism for candidates to address any concerns or complaints they may have regarding the interview process.

  Even with the best intentions, bias can sometimes creep into the interview process, leading to unfair treatment of candidates. A formal appeal process provides candidates with a way to address any perceived bias or discrimination, which can help to prevent future occurrences of bias and promote a more inclusive hiring process.

A formal appeal process can also increase transparency and accountability in the hiring process, which can help to build trust and confidence among candidates and employees. By providing a clear and transparent process for addressing bias, organizations can demonstrate their commitment to fairness and inclusivity, which can enhance their reputation and attract top talent.

Overall, having a formal appeal process is an important component of a comprehensive D&I strategy, as it can help to identify and address unconscious bias and promote a more inclusive workplace culture.
Here are a few steps that might be included in an appeal process for an interviewee to raise a complaint of bias:

- The appeal process needs to be transparent and communicated to all parties involved.
- This might include providing information about who is responsible for reviewing and addressing the complaint, and what steps will be taken to investigate the issue.
- Establish a clear process for interviewees to raise concerns about bias or discrimination. This might include providing information about how to report a complaint and whom to contact.
- Ensure the candidate is aware of the appeal process after, if not before the interview.

- Complaint email ID or contact details of the D&I committee to be placed in a visible area during the interview process. Email id can be reiterated in the email sent to the candidate confirming acceptance or rejection of the candidature.
- If you are using software for a candidate to upload their details, make sure it is placed at a noticeable placement.
- Ensure that there is a fair and unbiased process for reviewing and addressing complaints of bias. This might include having a separate team or individual responsible for reviewing and investigating the complaint. The appeal process should be fair and unbiased and should consider the perspectives of all parties involved. This might include providing an opportunity for the interviewee to present their concerns and any supporting evidence, and for the organization to respond to the complaint. It is important to ensure that the appeal process is confidential and that the privacy of all parties involved is protected. This might include limiting the number of people who are aware of the complaint and the outcome of the appeal process.
- Provide support and assistance to interviewees who have experienced bias, including information about their rights and options for addressing the issue.
- The appeal process should be timely, and steps should be taken to resolve the issue as quickly as possible. This might include setting deadlines for reviewing and addressing the complaint and providing regular updates to the interviewee about the status of the appeal.

○ The outcome of the appeal process should be communicated to the interviewee and any other relevant parties, and steps should be taken to resolve the issue to the satisfaction of all involved. This might include providing additional training or support to the recruitment team or taking disciplinary action against individuals who have engaged in biased behaviour.

So, now that we have seen how our personal biases can sometimes cloud our judgement to such an extent that we leave out high-performing or high-potential candidates, such labels and judgements penetrate across the veil on the selection process too. It impacts the way we interact with others on daily basis.

If remained unchecked, it can adversely affect the employee morale and productivity of our high-performing individuals who may even end up quitting the job when subjected to such discrimination and lack of empathy towards their circumstances.

Now with these new tools available in your arsenal, I am certain that you will be able to become an inclusive Hiring Manager. You will become a brand ambassador for your company to the outer world.

This will not only help you during the hiring process but these tips and strategies can also be used in any form of interview such as for promotions or performance assessments. These tools will certainly help you better navigate your interactions with co-workers and others in the workplace. Know that even the smallest effort has the potential to create a domino effect. Be the change you want to see.

CHAPTER SIX

Uncovering the Unconscious Bias: Talent Management

The role of leaders and managers in inclusive talent engagement and management is critical in creating an environment that values diversity, equity, and inclusion. Leaders and managers play a crucial role in developing and implementing strategies that ensure all employees feel valued, respected, and supported in their roles.

One of the key roles of leaders and managers is to create an inclusive culture that welcomes and celebrates diversity. They should be actively involved in recruiting and retaining a diverse workforce and provide equal opportunities for career advancement and development. They should also promote and reward inclusive behaviours, such as active listening, empathy, and open-mindedness while addressing any forms of discrimination or bias.

Leaders and managers should also be responsible for fostering a culture of belonging that empowers employees to contribute their unique perspectives and skills to the organization. This involves providing opportunities for feedback, recognition, and professional growth, as well as addressing any barriers that may impede employee engagement.

In short, there are no two thoughts that leaders and managers play a critical role in creating an inclusive workplace culture that values and supports diverse talent. By actively engaging with employees, promoting inclusive behaviours, and fostering a culture of belonging, leaders and managers can attract, retain, and develop top talent while driving business success. Leaders and managers play a critical role in creating and fostering an inclusive work environment, and in ensuring that talent engagement and management practices are inclusive and unbiased.

Here are a few specific ways in which leaders and managers can support inclusive talent engagement and management:

- Set clear diversity and inclusion goals and expectations for the organization and hold themselves and their teams accountable for meeting these goals.
- Leaders and managers should be proactive in promoting diversity and inclusion within their teams and the organization. This might include identifying and addressing any barriers to inclusion and taking steps to create a welcoming and inclusive environment for all employees.
- Leaders and managers should be aware of their own biases and try to minimize their impact on the recruitment and management process. This might include seeking out diverse candidates, using structured and consistent processes for evaluating and promoting employees, and seeking input and feedback from diverse stakeholders.

- Leaders and managers should be transparent about the organization's diversity and inclusion goals and efforts and should communicate these goals and efforts to employees at all levels. This can help to build trust and foster a culture of inclusion within the organization.
- Leaders and managers should be responsive to the needs and concerns of diverse employees and should work to create a supportive and inclusive work environment that values and respects the unique strengths and perspectives of all employees.
- Leaders and managers should be proactive in addressing any issues of bias or discrimination that may arise within their teams or the organization and should work to create a culture of respect and inclusion that promotes the success and well-being of all employees.

Employee Engagement and Productivity

Inclusive managers can have a positive impact on employee engagement and productivity by creating a work environment that values and respects the unique strengths and perspectives of all employees. When employees feel included and valued, they are more likely to be motivated and committed to their work and to contribute their full potential to the organization. Conversely, when employees feel excluded or discriminated against, they may be less engaged and motivated and may be less productive as a result.

Here are a few specific ways in which inclusive managers can impact employee engagement and productivity:

- By creating a welcoming and inclusive environment, inclusive managers can help to foster a sense of belonging and community among employees. This can lead to increased collaboration and teamwork, which can in turn increase productivity.

- Inclusive managers who value and respect the unique strengths and perspectives of all employees can help to create a positive work culture that is supportive and empowering. This can lead to increased motivation and engagement among employees.

- Inclusive managers who are proactive in addressing issues of bias or discrimination can help to create a fair and equitable work environment that promotes the success and well-being of all employees. This can lead to increased trust and commitment among employees and can contribute to increased productivity and engagement. By addressing issues of bias or discrimination when they arise, inclusive managers can help to create a fair and equitable work environment that promotes the success and well-being of all employees. This can lead to increased trust and commitment among employees and can contribute to increased productivity and engagement.

- Inclusive managers who communicate openly and transparently with their teams can help to build trust and create a sense of shared purpose and vision. This can lead to increased collaboration and teamwork and can contribute to increased productivity and engagement. By promoting open and honest communication, inclusive managers can create a culture of transparency and trust within the organization. This can lead to increased collaboration and teamwork, as employees feel that they can share their ideas and concerns openly and honestly.

- By providing opportunities for learning and development, inclusive managers can help to foster a culture of continuous improvement and growth within the organization. This can lead to increased motivation and engagement among employees, as they feel that they have opportunities to grow and advance within the organization.
- Inclusive managers who provide support and resources to help employees succeed in their roles can contribute to increased productivity and engagement. This might include providing training and development opportunities, offering support for work-life balance, or providing resources to help employees meet the demands of their roles.
- By recognizing and celebrating the contributions of all employees, inclusive managers can create a sense of appreciation and respect within the organization. This can lead to increased motivation and engagement, as employees feel that their efforts are valued and recognized.
- By promoting diversity and inclusion within their teams and the organization, the inclusive manager can create a more welcoming and inclusive work environment that values and respects the unique strengths and perspectives of all employees. This can lead to increased motivation and engagement, as employees feel that they are valued and included in the team.
- By providing opportunities for employees to contribute their ideas and feedback, inclusive managers can create a culture of collaboration and innovation within the organization. This can lead to increased motivation and engagement, as employees feel that their input is valued and that they have a voice in shaping the direction of the

organization.

- Inclusive managers who are supportive and approachable can create a positive work culture that is empowering and supportive. This can lead to increased motivation and engagement, as employees feel that they have a supportive and responsive leader who is committed to their success.

Work Assignments and Task Management

The role of leaders and managers in inclusive talent engagement and management when it comes to work assignments and task management is to ensure that everyone has equal opportunities to contribute their skills and expertise to the organization.

To accomplish this, leaders and managers should strive to create a work environment that is fair, transparent, and based on merit. They should provide employees with clear expectations, goals, and deadlines for their assignments, and communicate regularly to ensure that everyone is on the same page.

In addition, leaders and managers should take steps to ensure that work assignments are distributed fairly and that employees are given opportunities to work on projects that align with their strengths and interests. They should also be open to feedback and input from employees and encourage them to share their ideas and suggestions for improving work assignments and task management.

To promote inclusivity, leaders and managers should also be mindful of any potential biases or barriers that may impact work assignments and task management. They should strive to eliminate any unfair practices or favouritism and instead make decisions based on objective criteria such as skills, qualifications, and performance.

Overall, leaders and managers have a critical role to play in creating a workplace culture that values and supports diverse talent when it comes to work assignments and task management. By providing equal opportunities and promoting fairness and inclusivity, they can create a more engaged and productive workforce that drives business success.

Here are a few strategies that managers can use to remove gender bias when assigning work:

- Use objective criteria to determine the most qualified individual for a task, rather than relying on assumptions or personal preferences. This might include considering factors such as relevant skills and experience, past performance, and growth potential.
- Encourage the development of diverse and inclusive teams and seek out individuals from underrepresented groups for inclusion on teams for leadership roles.
- Foster a culture of respect and inclusion within the organization, and actively work to eliminate any barriers to inclusion. This might include providing accommodations for employees with disabilities, or specific gender requirements.
- Provide opportunities for learning and development to all employees, including those from underrepresented groups, to help them develop the skills and experience needed to succeed in their roles.
- Regularly review and assess the effectiveness of the work assignment process and adjust as needed to ensure that it is inclusive and unbiased. This might include seeking input and feedback from employees and other stakeholders and using data to identify any patterns of bias or inequality.

Performance Assessments and Promotion Decisions
The role of leaders and managers in inclusive talent engagement and management when it comes to performance assessments and promotion decisions is to ensure that these processes are fair, unbiased, and based on objective criteria.

Leaders and managers should establish clear performance metrics and goals that are transparent, measurable, and aligned with the organization's values and objectives. They should provide regular feedback and coaching to employees to help them improve their performance and achieve their goals.

In addition, leaders and managers should be mindful of any unconscious biases that may affect performance assessments and promotion decisions. They should ensure that evaluations are based on objective criteria such as job-related skills, knowledge, and behaviours, and not influenced by factors such as gender, ethnicity, age, or other personal characteristics.

Leaders and managers should also provide equal opportunities for employees to be considered for promotions and career advancement. They should encourage and support employees to develop their skills and knowledge through training, mentoring, and job rotations. They should also provide opportunities for employees to showcase their talents and contributions to the organization.

Overall, leaders and managers play a critical role in ensuring that performance assessments and promotion decisions are fair, objective, and unbiased. By providing equal opportunities for career development and advancement, they can create a more engaged and motivated workforce that contributes to the success of the organization.

Here are key points that a manager should keep in mind when doing a performance assessment or promotion discussion to avoid gender bias:

- Use structured, consistent processes for evaluating performance and making promotion decisions. This might include using objective criteria to assess performance, such as specific goals and objectives, and using a rating scale to ensure that evaluations are consistent and fair.
- Seek input and feedback from diverse stakeholders, including employees and community members, to ensure that the performance assessment and promotion process is fair and representative.
- Provide diversity and inclusion training to all employees, including managers, to help them understand the importance of diversity and how to avoid biases in the evaluation and promotion process.
- Regularly review and assess the effectiveness of the performance assessment and promotion process and adjust as needed to ensure that it is inclusive and unbiased.
- Address any issues of bias or discrimination that may arise during the performance assessment or promotion process and take appropriate action to resolve the issue and prevent future occurrences.

Importance of Documentation in Giving Employee Feedback

The role of leaders and managers in inclusive talent engagement and management when it comes to documentation in giving employee feedback is to ensure that feedback is objective, specific, and based on observable behaviours and that it is documented clearly and transparently.

Documentation is essential in giving employee feedback for several reasons. Firstly, it provides a record of performance over time, which can be used to identify patterns and trends, and to make more informed decisions about promotions, raises, and other career development opportunities. Secondly, it helps to ensure that feedback is consistent and fair and that all employees are held to the same standards. Finally, it provides a basis for legal defence in case of disputes or claims of discrimination or harassment.

Leaders and managers should document feedback using clear and specific language that describes the employee's performance objectively and accurately. They should avoid subjective language or judgments that may be influenced by personal biases or assumptions. They should also provide examples of specific behaviours or incidents that support their feedback, and avoid making generalizations or assumptions about the employee's performance.

In addition, leaders and managers should ensure that feedback is communicated in a timely and appropriate manner and that employees have an opportunity to respond and provide feedback of their own. They should also be open to constructive feedback from employees, and use this feedback to improve their own leadership and management skills.

Overall, the role of leaders and managers in inclusive talent engagement and management when it comes to documentation in giving employee feedback is to ensure that feedback is clear, specific, objective, and transparent and that it is used to support employee development and growth. By providing consistent and fair feedback, they can create a more engaged and motivated workforce that contributes to the success of the organization.

Documentation is important in giving employee feedback for several reasons:

- Documentation helps to ensure that feedback is accurate and fair. By documenting specific examples of an employee's performance, managers can provide more accurate and objective feedback, rather than relying on personal opinions or subjective impressions.
- Documentation can provide a record of an employee's performance and progress over time, which can be useful in making decisions about promotions, salary increases, and other career development opportunities.
- Documentation can help to ensure that feedback is consistent and unbiased. By using structured, consistent processes for documenting feedback, managers can avoid biases and ensure that all employees are treated fairly.
- Documentation can provide a reference point for future discussions about an employee's performance and development. By keeping a record of previous feedback, managers can more easily track an employee's progress and identify areas for improvement.
- Documentation can help to protect the organization against potential legal challenges related to performance evaluations and promotions. By keeping a record of the feedback and decisions made, the organization can demonstrate that they were based on objective criteria and were fair and unbiased.

Importance of Documented Employee Feedback in Malicious Complaints:

Documenting feedback for non-performance can help to protect a manager from a malicious complaint of sexual harassment or gender bias in several ways:

- By documenting specific examples of an employee's non-performance, a manager can demonstrate that the feedback was not based on personal biases or preferences, but on objective criteria related to the employee's job duties and responsibilities.

- Documentation can provide a record of the steps taken to address an employee's non-performance, which can help to demonstrate that the manager took appropriate action to address the issue and was not motivated by any personal biases or discriminatory attitudes.

- Documentation can help to demonstrate that the manager provided the employee with adequate support and resources to improve their performance and that any negative consequences (such as disciplinary action or termination) were based on the employee's failure to meet job expectations, rather than on any personal biases or discriminatory attitudes.

- By keeping a record of feedback and decisions related to non-performance, a manager can more easily defend themselves against a malicious complaint of sexual harassment or gender bias, as they will have a record of the objective criteria and processes used to evaluate and address the employee's performance.

- Managers need to document feedback for non-performance promptly, as this can help to demonstrate that any negative consequences (such as disciplinary action or termination) were based on the employee's current performance, rather than on any personal biases or discriminatory attitudes.

- Documentation should be objective and unbiased and should focus on specific examples of the employee's non-performance, rather than on personal opinions or subjective impressions.
- Managers need to provide ongoing support and resources to employees to help them improve their performance and to document these efforts to demonstrate that they took appropriate action to address any issues.
- Managers should be transparent and open in their communication with employees and should document any feedback or decisions related to non-performance clearly and concisely. This can help to build trust and understanding between the manager and the employee and can reduce the risk of a malicious complaint.
- The organization needs to have clear policies and procedures in place for addressing performance issues and providing support to employees, and for managers to follow these policies and procedures when giving feedback and addressing non-performance. This can help to ensure that the process is fair and unbiased and can protect against malicious complaints.

Inclusive Leadership

An inclusive leader is someone who values diversity and promotes inclusion within their organization or team. Inclusive leaders strive to create a welcoming and supportive work environment that values and respects the unique strengths and perspectives of all employees.

Inclusive leadership is a leadership style that prioritizes diversity, equity, and inclusion in decision-making, communication, and action. Inclusive leaders seek to create an environment where everyone feels valued, respected, and supported, regardless of their background, identity, or perspective.

Putting this into the context of leaders, inclusive leadership is about:

- Treating people and groups fairly—that is, based on their unique characteristics, rather than on stereotypes.
- Personalizing individuals—that is, understanding and valuing the uniqueness of diverse others while also accepting them as members of the group.
- Leveraging the thinking of diverse groups for smarter ideation and decision-making reduces the risk of being blindsided

An inclusive leader is someone who demonstrates the following qualities:

- **Self-awareness**: An inclusive leader is aware of their own biases, assumptions, and limitations, and is open to feedback and learning. To develop this quality, leaders can:

  - Take regular self-assessments to identify their own biases and assumptions.
  - Seek feedback from colleagues and team members to gain insight into how their behaviour and communication may be perceived.
  - Attend training and workshops on cultural competence, unconscious bias, and inclusive leadership.

- **Empathy:** An inclusive leader seeks to understand the experiences and perspectives of others and can communicate and connect with people from diverse backgrounds. To develop this quality, leaders can:

  - Practice active listening and ask open-ended questions to encourage dialogue and understanding.
  - Seek out opportunities to interact with people from different backgrounds, cultures, and experiences.
  - Attend training on empathy and emotional intelligence.

- **Cultural competence:** An inclusive leader has knowledge and understanding of different cultures and identities and can adapt their leadership style to accommodate diverse needs and perspectives. To develop this quality, leaders can:

  - Educate themselves on the history, values, and customs of different cultures.
  - Attend diversity and inclusion training to develop a deeper understanding of how to engage with people from diverse backgrounds.
  - Seek mentors or coaches who have experience working with diverse groups.

- **Courage:** An inclusive leader is willing to take risks, challenge the status quo, and speak out against discrimination, bias, and inequity. To develop this quality, leaders can:

  - Practice speaking up in situations where they witness discrimination, bias, or inequity.

- ∘ Educate themselves on issues of equity and inclusion and stay informed about current events.
- ∘ Build a support network of colleagues and mentors who share their values.

- **Collaboration:** An inclusive leader values teamwork and seeks to create a culture of collaboration and cooperation where everyone has a voice and can contribute to decision-making. To develop this quality, leaders can:

  - ∘ Create opportunities for team members to provide input and feedback on decisions and projects.
  - ∘ Encourage open communication and dialogue to foster a culture of transparency and trust.
  - ∘ Celebrate team successes and recognize the contributions of individual team members.

- **Accountability:** An inclusive leader takes responsibility for their actions and decisions and is willing to be held accountable for their impact on others. To develop this quality, leaders can:

  - ∘ Seek feedback and input from team members to gain insight into how their decisions and actions are perceived.
  - ∘ Take ownership of mistakes and seek to make amends or offer solutions.
  - ∘ Be transparent about decision-making processes and communicate clearly with team members.

- **Commitment:** An inclusive leader is committed to promoting diversity, equity, and inclusion in all aspects of their leadership and organizational culture, and is willing to invest time, resources, and effort to achieve this goal. To develop this quality, leaders can:

- Create a diversity and inclusion strategy that outlines goals, metrics, and action plans.
- Hold themselves and their team members accountable for promoting diversity, equity, and inclusion.
- Invest in training and development programs that promote diversity and inclusion.

The most important aspect of becoming an inclusive leader is empathy and cultural competence from my perspective.

Cultural competence is the ability to effectively communicate, interact, and work with individuals from different cultural backgrounds. In today's globalized world, cultural competence is becoming increasingly important for managers and leaders to successfully engage with their teams and create a culture of inclusivity. Cultural competence has four components: awareness, attitude, knowledge, and skills.

The first component of cultural competence is awareness. Awareness refers to the ability to recognize one's own cultural biases and assumptions and how they may affect interactions with individuals from different cultures. Managers and leaders can become more aware of their cultural biases and assumptions by:

- Engaging in self-reflection and introspection to recognize and address their own biases.

- Actively seeking out and listening to feedback from team members and colleagues from different cultural backgrounds.
- Participating in cultural competency training and development programs to increase awareness.

The second component of cultural competence is attitude. Attitude refers to having a positive and respectful attitude towards individuals from different cultural backgrounds. Managers and leaders can cultivate a positive attitude by:

- Recognizing the value and benefits of diversity and cultural differences within their team.
- Avoiding stereotypes and assumptions about individuals from different cultures.
- Encouraging team members to share their cultural experiences and perspectives.

The third component of cultural competence is knowledge. Knowledge refers to having a deep understanding of different cultural practices, beliefs, values, and norms. Managers and leaders can increase their cultural knowledge by:

- Learning about different cultural practices, beliefs, and values through research and reading.
- Engaging in cultural exchange programs and immersing themselves in different cultural experiences.
- Encouraging team members to share their cultural experiences and perspectives.

The fourth component of cultural competence skills. Skills refer to the ability to effectively communicate and interact with individuals from different cultural backgrounds. Managers and leaders can develop cultural skills by:

- Practising active listening and effective communication with individuals from different cultures.
- Adapting communication styles to accommodate cultural differences.
- Developing a cultural competency plan that outlines specific skills to be developed.

In conclusion, cultural competence is a crucial skill for managers and leaders to create an inclusive and diverse workplace. The four components of cultural competence - awareness, attitude, knowledge, and skills - are interrelated and require ongoing development to effectively work with individuals from different cultural backgrounds. Managers and leaders can improve their cultural competence by engaging in self-reflection, seeking out cultural knowledge, cultivating a positive attitude, and developing cultural skills.

Remember, D&I is not a destination, it is a journey for continual self-development. I look forward to connecting with you again.

CHAPTER SEVEN

Addressing the Workplace Bias in India

In recent years, India has made significant progress in creating a more inclusive workplace for women, transgender persons, and persons with disabilities. However, there is still a long way to go to ensure that these individuals receive equal opportunities and are protected from discrimination in the workplace.

The need for creating a psychologically safe workplace is becoming increasingly important in India due to the Transgender Persons (Protection of Rights) Bill, 2019 and the Rights of Persons with Disabilities Act, 2016. The Transgender Persons Bill mandates that every establishment that employs transgender persons should maintain a register of employment, provide safe working conditions, and prohibit any discrimination against them. It also requires employers to create a complaint mechanism to address any grievances raised by transgender employees. This has highlighted the need for managers to be aware of their unconscious biases and take steps to create a more inclusive and supportive workplace for transgender individuals.

Similarly, the Rights of Persons with Disabilities Act, 2016 requires employers to provide reasonable accommodations for persons with disabilities, create a barrier-free environment, and ensure equal opportunity in recruitment, promotion, and training. This underscores the importance of managers being mindful of their biases during recruitment, performance evaluations, and in providing accommodations for employees with disabilities. By creating a psychologically safe workplace, managers can ensure that employees from diverse backgrounds, including those who identify as transgender or have disabilities, feel valued and supported in their work environment. This can lead to higher productivity, better employee morale, and a more positive workplace culture.

Business Responsibility and Sustainability Reporting (BRSR) is an important framework that companies in India are expected to follow to ensure sustainable and responsible business practices. As part of BRSR, companies are required to disclose their policies and actions related to diversity and inclusion. This includes the steps taken to ensure equal opportunities for people from diverse backgrounds, and measures to combat any form of discrimination or bias.

BRSR emphasizes the importance of creating an inclusive workplace that promotes diversity and ensures that all employees feel valued and respected. Companies are expected to monitor and track their progress in terms of diversity and inclusion metrics, and take steps to address any gaps or areas of improvement. By incorporating D&I initiatives into their BRSR framework, companies can demonstrate their commitment to social responsibility and create a positive impact on society.

Thus, we see that creating a psychologically safe workplace is crucial for managers in India for several reasons. Firstly, a psychologically safe workplace enables employees to bring their whole selves to work, which leads to increased job satisfaction and engagement. When employees feel safe and valued, they are more likely to be creative and innovative, leading to better problem-solving and decision-making.

Secondly, a psychologically safe workplace promotes diversity and inclusion, making it easier to attract and retain talent from diverse backgrounds. This, in turn, leads to a more diverse and inclusive workplace culture, which is critical for success in today's global marketplace.

Thirdly, a psychologically safe workplace helps to reduce stress, anxiety, and burnout among employees, leading to better mental and physical health outcomes. This not only benefits employees but also enhances the overall productivity and performance of the organization.

Finally, creating a psychologically safe workplace is not only the right thing to do, but it is also essential to comply with various employment laws and regulations that prohibit discrimination and harassment based on gender, race, religion, and other protected characteristics.

One of the key steps that Indian organizations can take to address workplace bias is to create a Diversity and Inclusion Policy. This policy should lay out guidelines for fair recruitment, equal pay, and opportunities for career growth for individuals from diverse backgrounds. This policy should also outline the organization's commitment to creating a safe and inclusive workplace for all employees.

Equal employment opportunities are another important aspect of ensuring that workplace bias is addressed. All job openings should be advertised in a manner that reaches a diverse pool of candidates. Recruitment should be fair and transparent, and candidates should be evaluated based on their skills and experience rather than their gender, disability status, or other personal characteristics.

One of the most important aspects of addressing workplace bias for persons with disabilities is the provision of reasonable accommodation. The Right of Persons with Disabilities Act, 2016 mandates that employers provide reasonable accommodation to persons with disabilities. This may involve making physical modifications to the workplace or providing assistive technology to enable persons with disabilities to perform their job duties effectively.

Sensitization and awareness training are also essential for creating an inclusive workplace culture. These training programs can help employees understand the importance of diversity and inclusion and enable them to recognize and address workplace bias. Training may include topics such as gender sensitivity, disability awareness, and understanding transgender persons.

Anti-discrimination policies are another critical aspect of addressing workplace bias. Indian organizations can implement policies that prohibit discrimination and harassment in the workplace. These policies should be communicated clearly to all employees, and mechanisms for reporting incidents of discrimination or harassment should be put in place. It is also essential to ensure that employees who report such incidents are protected from retaliation.

Inclusive workplace practices are another important aspect of creating an inclusive workplace culture. These practices should be designed to cater to the needs of women, transgender persons, and persons with disabilities.

For example, providing flexible working hours, work from home options, or creating accessible workplaces can enable these individuals to perform their job duties effectively.

Finally, Indian organizations must comply with laws such as the Right of Persons with Disabilities Act, 2016 and the Transgender Persons (Protection of Rights) Bill, 2019, which mandate equal opportunities and protection from discrimination for persons with disabilities and transgender persons. Organizations should take steps to ensure that they are fully compliant with these laws to create a safe and inclusive workplace for all employees.

Conducting workplace audits, employee surveys, and establishing a strong grievance redressal mechanism are crucial steps that Indian organizations can take to address workplace bias.

Workplace audits can be conducted to identify potential areas of bias within an organization. An audit can assess whether the organization is complying with relevant laws and policies related to diversity and inclusion, and identify any practices or policies that may be creating barriers for women, transgender persons, and persons with disabilities. The audit should be conducted by an independent and qualified third party who can provide an objective assessment of the organization's current practices.

Employee surveys can be used to gather feedback from employees regarding their experiences of bias in the workplace. These surveys can help identify specific areas of concern and provide insights into the experiences of employees from diverse backgrounds. The survey results can be used to inform the organization's diversity and inclusion policies and practices.

Allyship is a crucial component in addressing workplace bias. Allies can use their privilege and influence to help create a more inclusive work environment. By actively supporting and advocating for those from marginalized or underrepresented groups, allies can help to promote equality and respect for diversity in the workplace. Allies can play a crucial role in calling out instances of bias, providing support to affected employees, and educating themselves about the experiences of others. ERGs can also play a role in educating others about the experiences of marginalized groups. By organizing events and activities, ERGs can help to raise awareness about the challenges faced by employees from diverse backgrounds. They can also provide training and education to other employees on topics such as cultural sensitivity, unconscious bias, and inclusive language.

Employee Resource Groups (ERGs) are another critical component in addressing workplace bias. ERGs are employee-led groups that focus on supporting employees from diverse backgrounds. These groups provide a safe space for employees to connect, share their experiences, and provide support to each other. ERGs can also help to identify areas of bias within the workplace and work with the organization to implement effective solutions.

ERGs can also help to promote diversity and inclusion within the organization. By partnering with HR and other departments, ERGs can advocate for policies and practices that promote diversity and inclusion. ERGs can also provide feedback on recruitment and hiring processes to ensure that they are fair and inclusive.

Establishing a strong grievance redressal mechanism is critical for addressing workplace bias. The mechanism should be accessible to all employees and provide a safe and confidential space for employees to report incidents of discrimination, harassment, or other forms of bias. The organization should ensure that employees who report incidents of bias are protected from retaliation and that the matter is investigated promptly and impartially. The mechanism should also include provisions for resolving grievances and providing remedies for affected employees.

To establish an effective grievance redressal mechanism, organizations can appoint a designated officer or committee responsible for handling complaints related to bias. The officer or committee should be trained to handle complaints sensitively and effectively. Additionally, the organization should ensure that employees are aware of the grievance redressal mechanism and know how to report incidents of bias.

Addressing workplace bias is a critical aspect of creating an inclusive workplace culture in India. Organizations can take several steps to address bias against women, transgender persons, and persons with disabilities, including creating a Diversity and Inclusion Policy, providing equal employment opportunities, providing reasonable accommodation, conducting sensitization and awareness training, implementing anti-discrimination policies, creating inclusive workplace practices, and complying with relevant laws. By taking these steps, Indian organizations can create a more inclusive and diverse workplace that caters to the needs of all employees, leading to a more productive and positive work environment.

Leading Indian organizations have taken significant steps to combat unconscious bias in the workplace under their D&I initiatives. Here are some examples of their efforts:

- **Tata Steel:** Tata Steel has launched a program called "Women of Mettle" to promote gender diversity and inclusivity in the workplace. The program offers training and development opportunities, mentorship, and networking opportunities to female employees. The company also has a policy of blind CVs to eliminate unconscious bias in the recruitment process.

- **IBM India:** IBM India has implemented several D&I initiatives, including "PRIDE," a network for LGBT+ employees, and "Women at IBM," a program that promotes gender diversity and provides career development opportunities for female employees. The company also uses a structured interview process to reduce unconscious bias in the recruitment process.

- **Accenture:** Accenture has a comprehensive D&I strategy that includes training programs for managers and employees to identify and address unconscious bias. The company also has employee resource groups (ERGs) for underrepresented groups, such as "Accenture Abilities" for employees with disabilities, and "Women's Network" for female employees.

- **Infosys:** Infosys has implemented several initiatives to promote gender diversity and inclusion, including "Infosys Women's Inclusivity Network" (IWIN), which offers career development opportunities and mentorship for female employees. The company also provides unconscious bias training for managers and has implemented a policy of blind recruitment.

- **Wipro:** Wipro has a "Women of Wipro" initiative that aims to increase the representation of women in leadership roles. The company also has an "AbilityWipro" program to promote disability inclusion in the workplace. The company's recruitment process includes a diversity dashboard to track the diversity of candidates.

- **HCL Technologies:** HCL Technologies has implemented several initiatives to promote diversity and inclusion, including "Diversity and Inclusion Councils" and "Employee Resource Groups" for underrepresented groups. The company also provides unconscious bias training for hiring managers and uses a structured interview process to reduce bias in the recruitment process.
- **Godrej Group:** Godrej Group has a comprehensive D&I strategy that includes training programs for managers and employees to identify and address unconscious bias. The company has implemented a policy of blind CVs and uses a structured interview process to reduce bias in the recruitment process.
- **Mahindra Group:** Mahindra Group has implemented several initiatives to promote diversity and inclusion, including "Women Leaders' Council" and "Mahindra Diversity Council." The company also has an "All Abilities" program to promote disability inclusion in the workplace.
- **Hindustan Unilever Limited:** Hindustan Unilever Limited has a "Diversity and Inclusion" strategy that includes several initiatives to promote gender diversity and inclusion. The company has implemented a policy of blind CVs and uses a structured interview process to reduce bias in the recruitment process.
- **Cognizant:** Cognizant has a comprehensive D&I strategy that includes training programs for managers and employees to identify and address unconscious bias. The company also has employee resource groups (ERGs) for underrepresented groups, such as "Pride@Cognizant" for LGBT+ employees, and "Women Empowered" for female employees. The company has

also implemented a policy of blind CVs to reduce unconscious bias in the recruitment process.

These organizations combat unconscious bias in the workplace by implementing policies and initiatives that promote diversity and inclusion, offering training programs for managers and employees, implementing blind CVs and structured interview processes, and providing career development opportunities and support for underrepresented groups.

Thus, we witness that there is certainly a need to conduct workplace audits, employee surveys, and establishing a strong grievance redressal mechanism are critical steps that Indian organizations can take to address workplace bias. By implementing these measures, organizations can identify potential areas of bias, gather feedback from employees, and create a safe and inclusive workplace for all employees. These measures, when combined with other diversity and inclusion initiatives, can help create a positive and productive work environment that values diversity and empowers all employees to achieve their full potential.

Ultimately, creating a psychologically safe and inclusive workplace requires a commitment from everyone in the organization. It requires a willingness to acknowledge and address unconscious bias and a dedication to promoting diversity, equity, and inclusion.

As managers and leaders, we have the responsibility to create a workplace culture that values diversity and empowers all employees to reach their full potential. By taking action to address unconscious bias and promoting inclusion, we can create a workplace where everyone feels valued, respected, and supported. Let us take this journey together and work towards building a brighter future for ourselves and our colleagues.

CHAPTER EIGHT

25 Self-Help Exercises For Managers

And as I always say, it all starts with 'me'.

By doing these exercises, individuals, managers and organizations can begin to address the unconscious biases that may be impacting their workplace culture. These biases can lead to discrimination and exclusion, which can have a negative impact on employee morale, productivity, and ultimately the success of the organization. It is important for managers and employees to recognize and interrupt these biases in order to create a psychologically safe and inclusive workplace where everyone feels valued and supported.

Moreover, the benefits of addressing unconscious biases go beyond just creating a more inclusive workplace. Studies have shown that diverse teams outperform homogeneous ones in terms of innovation, problem-solving, and decision-making. By cultivating a culture of diversity and inclusion, organizations can tap into the strengths of all employees and create a competitive advantage in the marketplace. Ultimately, taking these exercises seriously can not only create a more just and equitable workplace, but it can also lead to increased business success.

Here are 20 easy yet impactful self-help exercises that managers can do on their own to uncover and address their unconscious biases:

1. **Exercise 1: Mindful Breathing** - Set aside a few minutes each day for mindful breathing. Sit comfortably with your eyes closed and focus on your breath, allowing thoughts and emotions to come and go without judgment. This exercise can help you become more aware of your thoughts and feelings, which can reveal biases you may not have been aware of.

2. **Exercise 2: Reflect on Childhood Experiences** - Take some time to reflect on your childhood experiences and identify any instances where you may have been exposed to biases or stereotypes. Think about how these experiences may have influenced your own biases and beliefs, and consider how they may be affecting your decision-making in the workplace.

3. **Exercise 3: Identify Biases in the Workplace** - Take a critical look at your workplace and identify any biases that may exist. For example, are there certain employees who are consistently passed over for promotions? Do you tend to favour certain team members over others? By identifying these biases, you can take steps to address them and create a more equitable workplace.

4. **Exercise 4: Role Play** - Imagine a scenario in which you may be unconsciously biased and role-play the situation. For example, if you tend to favour extroverted employees over introverted ones, imagine a situation in which an introverted employee presents an idea that you initially dismiss. Role-play the situation, and consider how you might handle it differently to address your bias.

5. **Exercise 5: Mindful Listening** - Practice mindful listening by giving your full attention to the speaker in a conversation. Avoid distractions and truly listen to what they are saying, without making assumptions or judgments. After the conversation, reflect on any biases that may have come up during the conversation, and consider how you can be more open to diverse perspectives.

6. **Exercise 6: Analyze Media Consumption** - Take a critical look at the media you consume, including news, TV shows, movies, and social media. Identify any patterns or biases in the content you consume and consider how they may be shaping your views of certain groups or individuals.

7. **Exercise 7: Challenge Stereotypes** - Identify any stereotypes you hold about certain groups or individuals, and challenge them. For example, if you tend to stereotype older workers as less capable, seek out examples of older workers who are successful and accomplished.

8. **Exercise 8: Seek Out Diverse Perspectives** - Make an effort to seek out diverse perspectives and experiences. This can include reading books or articles written by people from different backgrounds, attending events or workshops that focus on diversity and inclusion, or seeking out friendships with people who have different experiences and perspectives.

9. **Exercise 9: Conduct a Bias Inventory** - Take an inventory of your own biases by identifying instances where you may have acted on or expressed biases. Write them down and reflect on how they may have impacted others. Use this inventory to guide your efforts to address your biases and create a more inclusive

workplace.

10. **Exercise 10: Practice Empathy** - Practice putting yourself in other people's shoes and considering their experiences and perspectives. This can help you become more aware of your own biases and develop a greater sense of empathy and understanding for others.

11. **Exercise 11: Conduct a Diversity Audit** - Assess the current state of diversity and inclusion within your team or organization. Identify areas where there may be a lack of diversity and consider strategies to address these gaps.

12. **Exercise 12: Use Gender-Neutral Language** - Be mindful of using gender-neutral language in your communications and avoid making assumptions about gender or gender identity.

13. **Exercise 13: Implement Blind Hiring** - Implement a blind hiring process that removes identifying information, such as names and photos, from resumes and applications to reduce the impact of unconscious bias in the hiring process.

14. **Exercise 14: Share Your Pronouns** - Share your own pronouns (e.g. she/her, he/him, they/them) and encourage others to do the same to create a more inclusive workplace for transgender and non-binary colleagues.

15. **Exercise 15: Identify Microaggressions** - Learn to recognize and interrupt microaggressions, which are subtle, often unintentional actions or comments that can reinforce stereotypes and marginalize others.

16. **Exercise 16: Encourage Open Dialogue** - Create opportunities for open dialogue and discussion around issues related to diversity and inclusion. Encourage employees to share their experiences and perspectives.

17. **Exercise 17: Challenge Unconscious Bias** - Be mindful of situations where unconscious bias may be at play, such as in performance evaluations or feedback discussions. Challenge these biases by actively seeking out diverse perspectives and questioning assumptions.
18. **Exercise 18: Advocate for Diversity and Inclusion** - Become an advocate for diversity and inclusion within your organization. Speak up about the importance of creating an inclusive workplace and support initiatives that promote diversity.
19. **Exercise 19: Learn About Other Cultures** - Educate yourself about different cultures and customs to develop a greater understanding and appreciation for diversity.
20. **Exercise 20: Celebrate Differences** - Create opportunities to celebrate diversity within your team or organization, such as hosting cultural events or recognizing important holidays and observances.

These exercises can help managers become more aware of their unconscious biases and take steps to address them. The mindfulness exercises can help managers become more present and centred, allowing them to approach the topic of bias with greater openness and empathy. The other exercises are designed to identify and challenge biases that may exist in the workplace or personal experiences, providing practical steps to promote a more inclusive and equitable workplace culture.

Here are five additional exercises that can help managers explore their childhood schemas and biases, and develop greater self-awareness and empathy for others in the workplace. It's important to approach this work with an open mind and a willingness, to be honest with yourself, even when it's uncomfortable. By doing so, you can become a more effective and inclusive leader, creating a more positive and productive workplace for everyone:

Exercise 21:Timeline exercise- Create a timeline of your life, marking significant events from childhood to the present. Reflect on each event and identify any experiences that may have contributed to the development of your biases. Ask yourself: What happened during this event? How did it make me feel? What did I learn from it? How might this be shaping my biases today?

Exercise 22: Journaling exercise- Take some time to reflect on your childhood experiences and write about any memories or feelings that come up. Consider how these experiences may have shaped your beliefs and biases today. Ask yourself: What messages did I receive from my family, friends, and community about different groups of people? How did I internalize these messages? How are these biases impacting my interactions with colleagues and employees in the workplace?

Exercise 23: Cognitive Behavioral Therapy (CBT) exercise- CBT is a type of therapy that helps people identify and change negative thought patterns. Apply this to your biases by identifying the negative thoughts and beliefs you hold about certain groups of people. Then, challenge these beliefs by asking yourself: Is this belief based on facts or assumptions? What evidence do I have to support this belief? Is there an alternative explanation or perspective that I haven't considered?

Exercise 24:Visualization exercise- Take some time to visualize a situation in the workplace where your biases may be influencing your behaviour. Picture yourself in the situation and reflect on your thoughts and feelings. Then, try to visualize a different outcome where your biases are not present. Ask yourself: How would I act differently in this situation if my biases weren't present? What would be the benefits of this different approach?

Exercise 25: Mindfulness exercise- Mindfulness is the practice of being fully present and aware of your thoughts, feelings, and sensations in the present moment, without judgment. Apply mindfulness to your biases by taking some time each day to sit quietly and observe your thoughts and feelings without trying to change them. As biases arise, simply acknowledge them and let them go. Reflect on how these biases may be impacting your behavior and interactions with others in the workplace. Ask yourself: What emotions and physical sensations am I experiencing? How are these biases influencing my thoughts and actions? How can I respond to situations in a more mindful and inclusive way?

These exercises can help you become more aware of your own unconscious biases and take steps to address them. By actively engaging in these exercises and reflecting on your own biases, you can work towards creating a more inclusive and equitable workplace culture.

Join us for our online training program on addressing workplace bias where we dive deeper into case studies, white papers and business scenarios for real-life solutions. Visit www.diversityandinclusion.in

CHAPTER NINE

Designing a Training Program on Uncovering the Unconscious Bias at Workplace

Training programs on uncovering unconscious bias in the workplace are essential for organizations to create a more inclusive work culture. Unconscious bias can lead to discrimination, which can negatively affect employee morale, productivity, and retention. By addressing unconscious bias, organizations can foster a more diverse and inclusive workplace, which can lead to better decision-making, innovation, and improved business outcomes.

The benefits of such training programs include increased awareness and understanding of unconscious bias, the ability to recognize and mitigate it, improved teamwork and collaboration, and enhanced employee engagement and job satisfaction. However, it is important to note that these programs may have some potential pitfalls. For example, if not executed well, they may be perceived as tokenistic or a box-ticking exercise. It is important to ensure that the training is well-designed, engaging, and relevant to the organization's goals and values.

When designing a training program on uncovering unconscious bias, it is essential to include modules on understanding unconscious bias and its impact, recognizing and addressing personal biases, understanding the role of privilege and power dynamics, and building inclusive practices and behaviours. The training should also provide practical strategies and tools to mitigate unconscious bias, such as blind recruitment, diverse hiring panels, and inclusive language in job postings.

It is important to avoid using a one-size-fits-all approach and instead tailor the training to the specific needs and culture of the organization. Additionally, it is important to avoid creating a culture of fear or blame, which may lead to defensive behaviour and resistance to change. Instead, the training should be framed positively, as an opportunity for personal and organizational growth and development.

Thus, designing a comprehensive training program on uncovering unconscious bias at the workplace is a critical step for organizations to foster a more inclusive and equitable work environment. It requires thoughtful planning, implementation, and evaluation to ensure that the program is effective and achieves the desired outcomes.

Important Considerations:

Designing a training program on uncovering unconscious bias at the workplace requires careful planning and implementation to ensure that it is effective in achieving the desired outcomes. Here are some key steps to consider:

- Identify the training objectives: The first step in designing the training program is to identify the objectives. The objectives should be specific, measurable, and achievable. For example, the objective of the training program could be to help managers and employees understand their unconscious biases and learn how to minimize their impact on decision-making.
- Conduct a needs analysis: Conducting a needs analysis helps in understanding the current state of the organization with respect to diversity and inclusion. This analysis can be done through surveys, interviews, and focus groups. It will help in identifying the areas where unconscious bias may be present and needs to be addressed.
- Develop the content: The training content should be designed to meet the identified training objectives. It should cover topics such as understanding unconscious bias, how to identify it, and strategies to overcome it. The training should also include case studies, real-life examples, and interactive exercises to engage participants and make the training more effective.
- Select the training method: The training method should be selected based on the training objectives and the needs of the organization. The training can be delivered through e-learning, classroom sessions, workshops, or a combination of these methods. The method selected should be engaging and interactive, to maximize the learning experience.
- Choose the trainers: The trainers should be carefully selected, and they should have the required knowledge and expertise in the area of diversity and inclusion. The

trainers should also be skilled in facilitating training sessions and engaging participants.

- Evaluate the training: Evaluation is an essential step in measuring the effectiveness of the training program. The evaluation should be conducted immediately after the training, and then periodically thereafter, to ensure that the training is having the desired impact. The feedback received can be used to make any necessary adjustments to the training program.

Overall, the training program should be designed to create awareness and provide practical strategies to help managers and employees uncover and address unconscious bias in the workplace. By creating a more inclusive workplace, organizations can benefit from increased creativity, innovation, and collaboration, which can lead to improved productivity and business outcomes.

Here's a sample course curriculum that can be designed for managers to counter unconscious bias at the workplace against employees from diverse backgrounds:

- Introduction to unconscious bias

  - Definition of unconscious bias
  - Impact of unconscious bias on the workplace
  - Recognizing personal biases

- Understanding diverse backgrounds

  - Different dimensions of diversity
  - Challenges faced by employees from diverse backgrounds
  - Stereotyping and its impact

- Recruitment and hiring practices

  - Unconscious bias in recruitment and hiring
  - Best practices for fair and inclusive recruitment
  - Understanding the importance of diverse sourcing and outreach

- Inclusive onboarding and training

  - Creating a welcoming and inclusive onboarding experience
  - Ensuring equitable access to training and development opportunities
  - Addressing unconscious bias in performance evaluations

- Managing and leading diverse teams

  - Understanding the importance of diversity in teams
  - Promoting inclusive leadership behaviors
  - Addressing conflicts and misunderstandings in diverse teams

- Building an inclusive workplace culture

  - Creating an inclusive workplace culture that values diversity
  - Addressing unconscious bias in organizational policies and practices
  - Encouraging employee engagement and participation in D&I initiatives

- Mitigating bias in career advancement and compensation

  ○ Identifying and mitigating bias in promotion and compensation decisions
  ○ Ensuring equitable access to career advancement opportunities
  ○ Developing and implementing fair and inclusive compensation policies

- Addressing unconscious bias in employee relations

  ○ Creating a respectful and inclusive work environment
  ○ Addressing bias and discrimination in the workplace
  ○ Developing a grievance redressal mechanism for employees to report incidents of bias

- Developing personal action plans

  ○ Reflecting on personal biases and areas for growth
  ○ Developing a personal action plan for addressing unconscious bias
  ○ Committing to ongoing learning and growth in diversity and inclusion

- Conclusion and evaluation

  ○ Review of key concepts and learning objectives
  ○ Evaluation of the training program
  ○ Commitment to ongoing support for diversity and inclusion initiatives in the workplace.

The adult learning methodology is essential in designing an effective training program for uncovering unconscious bias in the workplace. It involves creating an interactive and engaging learning environment that encourages managers to explore their biases, reflects on their actions and beliefs, and develop skills to overcome unconscious biases. The following are some examples of case studies and exercises that can be incorporated into the training program:

- Case Studies: Use real-life examples of bias incidents that have happened in the organization or industry to facilitate discussion and identify areas where unconscious bias might exist.
- Role-Playing: Have participants role-play different scenarios where unconscious bias might come into play, such as a job interview or performance evaluation.
- Group Discussions: Create a safe space for open discussions among participants to share their experiences and perspectives on unconscious bias in the workplace.
- Stereotype Analysis: Use media and popular culture examples to analyze stereotypes and their effects on the workplace.
- Mindfulness Exercises: Incorporate mindfulness exercises to help participants become more aware of their thoughts, feelings, and biases.
- Implicit Association Test (IAT): Use the IAT to help participants identify their own unconscious biases and discuss strategies to address them.
- Diversity and Inclusion Quizzes: Incorporate quizzes to test participants' knowledge of diversity and inclusion topics and reinforce key concepts covered in the training.

- Storytelling: Encourage participants to share their personal experiences with unconscious bias in the workplace and how they have addressed them.
- Empathy Building: Use empathy-building exercises to help participants better understand the experiences and perspectives of people from diverse backgrounds.
- Accountability Planning: Create an accountability plan for participants to commit to specific actions they will take to address unconscious bias in their workplace.

It is essential to avoid activities that may trigger emotional responses or reinforce negative stereotypes. The facilitator must create a safe and inclusive learning environment that encourages open and honest dialogue. Without a trained D&I facilitator, the training program can fall back onto the organization, resulting in negative consequences such as increased bias and discrimination. A trained D&I facilitator can navigate sensitive questions, provide context, and ensure that the training program meets the specific needs of the organization.

Having a trained D&I facilitator is essential to address sensitive subjects related to uncovering unconscious bias in the workplace. Sensitive subjects such as race, gender, sexuality, and disability can evoke strong emotions and require a safe and inclusive space for discussion. A trained facilitator can create such a space by establishing ground rules, ensuring everyone's voices are heard, and guiding the conversation in a respectful and productive manner.

If the facilitator is not fully equipped to address sensitive questions during the program, the training can fall back on the organization in several ways. Firstly, participants may feel unsupported and unheard, leading to a lack of trust in the organization's commitment to D&I.

Secondly, insensitive comments or behaviours can occur during the training, leading to negative feelings and potentially harmful impacts on the workplace culture. Finally, the organization may miss out on valuable insights and opportunities for growth if the training is not conducted in a safe and inclusive space. Sometimes the organization may be held responsible by the historically excluded groups to be creating more disparity and discrimination and may even invite legal complications.

Thus, having a trained D&I facilitator is crucial to ensuring that sensitive subjects related to uncovering unconscious bias are discussed in a safe and inclusive space. If the facilitator is not fully equipped to address sensitive questions during the program, it can have negative impacts on the workplace culture and the organization's commitment to D&I.

For more details, visit www.diversityandinclusion.in.

Epilogue

As you finish reading "Uncovering the Unconscious Bias: A Practical Guide for Managers to Create a Psychologically Safe and Inclusive Workplace," I want to leave you with some final thoughts and reflections on the important work of addressing unconscious bias and creating a truly inclusive workplace.

First and foremost, it is important to acknowledge that this work is not easy. It requires courage, vulnerability, and a willingness to confront uncomfortable truths about us and our organizations. It requires us to challenge deeply ingrained beliefs and behaviours and to make difficult decisions that may be met with resistance.

But despite these challenges, the work of addressing unconscious bias and creating an inclusive workplace is essential. We know that diversity, equity, and inclusion are not only moral imperatives but also critical to the success of organizations in today's global and interconnected world. A workplace that is not inclusive is not only unjust, but also inefficient, ineffective, and ultimately unsustainable.

To create a psychologically safe and inclusive workplace, we must approach this work with a sense of humility and curiosity. We must be willing to learn from those who have experiences and perspectives different from our own and recognize that our own biases and blind spots may be limiting our ability to see the full picture.

We must also recognize that creating an inclusive workplace is not a one-size-fits-all endeavour. Every organization, every team, and every individual is unique, and the strategies and tactics that work in one context may not work in another. Therefore, we must be flexible and adaptive, and willing to experiment and iterate as we go.

Finally, we must remember that this work is not just the responsibility of managers and leaders. Every employee has a role to play in creating an inclusive workplace, and it is only through collective action and shared commitment that we can truly make progress.

I hope that this book has provided you with some practical tools and strategies for addressing unconscious bias and creating a more inclusive workplace. But more importantly, I hope that it has sparked a deeper sense of curiosity, empathy, and commitment to this important work. The road ahead may be challenging, but it is also full of opportunity and possibility. I invite you to join me on this journey and to continue to learn, grow, and create change in your own workplace and beyond by connecting with me at www.diversityandinclusion.in.

Afterword

As you come to the end of this book, "Uncovering the Unconscious Bias: A Practical Guide for Managers to Create a Psychologically Safe and Inclusive Workplace," I hope that you feel empowered to act and make positive changes in your workplace. You have learned about the impact of unconscious bias on individuals and organizations, and how it can create barriers to achieving diversity, equity, and inclusion.

It is important to recognize that unconscious bias is not something that can be eliminated entirely. However, by increasing awareness and taking intentional steps to mitigate the effects of bias, we can create a more inclusive workplace where everyone feels valued and supported.

As a manager, you have a unique responsibility to lead by example and create a culture of inclusivity. This means being intentional about your actions, your language, and your decisions. It means seeking out diverse perspectives and experiences and being open to feedback and learning.

It also means recognizing that creating an inclusive workplace is an ongoing process, one that requires commitment and effort from everyone involved. It is not a quick fix or a one-time project, but rather a long-term commitment to creating a workplace where everyone can thrive.

I encourage you to continue learning and growing in your understanding of unconscious bias and its impact on the workplace. Seek out resources, attend training and workshops, and engage in conversations with colleagues and employees.

Together, we can create workplaces that are not only more inclusive but also more innovative, productive, and successful. Thank you for joining me on this journey, and I wish you all the best in your efforts to create a psychologically safe and inclusive workplace.

References & Acknowledgement

- "Managing Unconscious Bias" by Harvard Business Review
- "Diversity and Inclusion: The Reality Gap" by Deloitte
- "Race, Ethnicity, and Equality of Opportunity" by McKinsey & Company
- "The Business Case for Diversity and Inclusion" by Harvard Business Review
- "How Diversity Can Drive Innovation" by Harvard Business Review
- "Why Diversity Matters" by McKinsey & Company
- "Diversity Matters" by Catalyst
- "Unconscious Bias in Hiring" by Harvard Business Review
- "Making the Business Case for Diversity and Inclusion" by Deloitte
- "Inclusion at Work: The View from Silicon Valley" by Harvard Business Review
- "The Diversity and Inclusion Revolution: Eight Powerful Truths" by Deloitte
- "The Inclusion Imperative" by Harvard Business Review
- "Race and Ethnicity in the Workplace" by Deloitte
- "Diversity and Inclusion in the Asia Pacific" by McKinsey & Company
- "Racial Diversity: A Work in Progress" by Harvard Business Review
- "The Role of Men in Gender Diversity" by McKinsey & Company
- "Overcoming Bias: Building Authentic Relationships across Differences" by Harvard Business Review

- "The Diversity Dividend" by McKinsey & Company
- "Why Inclusive Leaders Are Good for Organizations, and How to Become One" by Harvard Business Review
- "Diversity and Inclusion: A Guide for Leaders" by Deloitte
- "The Business of Inclusion" by McKinsey & Company
- "How to Combat Unconscious Bias" by Harvard Business Review
- "Diversity Matters: Creating a More Inclusive Workplace" by McKinsey & Company
- "The Costs of Code-Switching" by Harvard Business Review
- "Inclusion, Diversity, and Equity in the Workplace" by Deloitte
- "Diversity and Inclusion: A Framework for Success" by McKinsey & Company
- "The Two Factors That Determine Whether Diversity Initiatives Succeed" by Harvard Business Review
- "Leading for Equity, Diversity, and Inclusion" by Deloitte
- "Diversity and Inclusion in the Boardroom" by McKinsey & Company
- "The Business Case for Racial Equity" by Harvard Business Review
- "The Future of Workplace Diversity Is Here, and It's Not What You Think" by Deloitte
- "The Hidden Biases in Hiring" by McKinsey & Company
- "What Makes a Successful Diversity and Inclusion Initiative?" by Harvard Business Review
- "Cultural Competence in the Workplace" by Deloitte
- "Diversity and Inclusion: A Business Imperative" by McKinsey & Company
- "The Leader's Guide to Unconscious Bias" by Harvard

Business Review
- "Gender Diversity and Corporate Performance" by McKinsey & Company
- "Diversity and Inclusion in the Digital Age" by Deloitte
- "The Business Case for Gender Diversity" by Harvard Business Review
- "Creating a Culture of Inclusion" by McKinsey & Company
- "The Costs of Racism for Individuals and Society" by Harvard Business Review
- American Psychological Association: "Cultural competence in health care: A review of the literature"
- Harvard Business Review: "Why diversity programs fail"
- Society for Human Resource Management: "Building cultural competence in the workplace."
- "Inclusion at Work: The View from Silicon Valley" by Harvard Business Review
- "The Inclusion Imperative" by Harvard Business Review
- "Diversity and Inclusion in the Asia Pacific" by McKinsey & Company
- "The Role of Men in Gender Diversity" by McKinsey & Company
- "Leading for Equity, Diversity, and Inclusion" by Deloitte.

Books By This Author

1. Cracking the Code of D&I: A practical guide to leveraging diversity and inclusion for organizational excellence.
2. The Ultimate D&I Strategy: Crafting a Comprehensive D&I Strategic Plan for Organizational Success.